AF761334

Safety and Risk in Society

nova
science publishers

www.novapublishers.com

Safety and Risk in Society

An Essential Guide to Occupational Exposure
Marta Madalena Marques de Oliveira, PhD,
Simone Barreira Morais, PhD,
Francisca Pinto Lisboa Martins Rodrigues, PhD (Editors)
2022. ISBN: 978-1-68507-819-5 (Hardcover)
2022. ISBN: 978-1-68507-922-2 (eBook)

Sexual Harassment and Assault in Government Agencies
Margaret Brown (Editor)
2021. ISBN: 978-1-53619-576-7 (Hardcover)
2021. ISBN: 978-1-53619-591-0 (eBook)

Sexual Harassment on Campus, at Work and in STEM Research
Jennifer Powell (Editor)
2021. ISBN: 978-1-53619-575-0 (Hardcover)
2021. ISBN: 978-1-53619-590-3 (eBook)

Hate Crimes in the United States
Joseph Pelletier (Editor)
2021. ISBN: 978-1-53619-325-1 (Hardcover)
2021. ISBN: 978-1-53619-360-2 (eBook)

Adolescent Dating Violence: Outcomes, Challenges and Digital Tools
Maria Alzira Pimenta Dinis,
Sónia Maria Martins Caridade (Editors)
2020. ISBN: 978-1-53617-479-3 (Softcover)
2020. ISBN: 978-1-53617-480-9 (eBook)

More information about this series can be found at
https://novapublishers.com/product-category/series/safety-and-risk-in-society/

Michael R. Weisser

Why Do (Some) Americans Love Their Guns?

Questions and Answers from Both Sides

nova
science publishers
New York

DOI: https://doi.org/10.52305/RQOA7082

Library of Congress Cataloging-in-Publication Data

Names: Weisser, Michael R., author.
Title: Why do (some) Americans love their guns? : questions and answers from both sides / Michael R. Weisser.
Description: New York : Nova Science Publishers, [2022] | Series: Safety and risk in society | Includes bibliographical references and index. |
Identifiers: LCCN 2022049838 (print) | LCCN 2022049839 (ebook) | ISBN 9798886972023 (paperback) | ISBN 9798886973730 (adobe pdf)
Subjects: LCSH: Gun control--United States. | Firearms ownership--United States. | Gun control--United States,
Classification: LCC HV7436 .W456 2022 (print) | LCC HV7436 (ebook) | DDC 363.330973--dc23/eng/20221123
LC record available at https://lccn.loc.gov/2022049838
LC ebook record available at https://lccn.loc.gov/2022049839

Published by Nova Science Publishers, Inc. † New York

To:

Carolyn
Leonard
Bernard
Seymour
Elsie

Contents

Introduction: Why This Book

Some years ago, I interviewed sixty-one boys, ages 14 – 17 years old, who were inmates in a youth jail. The state where this jail is located tries very hard to provide alternate programs for youthful offenders to keep them from becoming more delinquent because of their experiences behind bars. Only after a youngster has been unable to adjust to more benign forms of punishment does he wind up in this jail.[1]

The kids I interviewed had been convicted of serious crimes – murder, arson, drug dealing, aggravated assault - and would be transferred to one of the state penitentiaries when they turned eighteen. Notwithstanding their age, many of them were already career criminals and they knew that when their prison terms were finished, they would go right back to street life.

Many of these youngsters were Hispanic, and I speak Spanish as well as I speak English, so we had no difficulty communicating in one or another tongue. They knew I was a 'gun guy' because I sold guns to some of the guards, which is how I was able to arrange these interviews in the first place. I also was allowed to talk to the kids without a guard in the room so the interviews could be as candid as I wanted them to be.

I never published an account of these interviews because I would have first been required to get approval from the State Board of Corrections institutional review board, the IRB. This process would have taken years because since my interview subjects were minors, the IRB could only approve these interviews if the parents or guardians of the interviewees would consent to their charges being the subjects of my research. The parents or guardians of these kids had long ago disappeared.

But I wasn't interested in conducting these interviews because I wanted to write them up and publish the text in a scholarly journal. My motivation was simply to get some idea about what these young men thought about guns. In fact, along with serious felonies which landed them behind bars, just about all my interview subjects had also been caught with an illegal gun.

The discussions between me and the jail kids usually went about 30 minutes, and much of the time was spent in a relaxed give-and-take about whatever was on their minds. But I did ask all of them two questions and what follows are those questions and the usual response:

> Question #1: How hard is it to get your hands on a gun? Response: [Laughter.] "Guns are all around."
>
> Question #2: Why do you need to carry a gun? Response: "To protect myself. Why else?"

At some point during the time when I conducted these interviews, I happened to be in my gun shop getting ready to drive over to the jail when a guy in his mid-50's walked in looking to buy a Glock 17. This is the gun carried by more cops in the United States than any other gun. It was designed as a gun for military and law-enforcement use. In other words, it's not a 'sporting' gun.

The customer told me he wanted to buy this gun because he was getting worried about personal security and along with the gun, he wanted to buy several extra hi-capacity mags. He had the standard state-issued gun license which allowed him to walk around with the gun on his person concealed. My state has no limits on the number of handgun or rifle magazines you can carry around with or without a gun.

When I told him I didn't have the gun in stock but could probably order one that would be delivered in two or three days, he said he would drive down to the next town and if the gun shop in that town had the gun in its inventory, he would buy the gun there. Otherwise, he would call me, and I could order the gun for him. I don't recall who ended up selling him the gun.

I left the shop a few minutes later and as I was driving over to the youth jail it occurred to me that this customer, as law-abiding and well behaved as any adult could be, had basically said exactly the same thing about having a gun that a hardened and violent young criminal would say to me when I interviewed him later that day. After all, both of them knew that they could easily get their hands on a gun. And they also both wanted a gun to protect themselves from somebody else.

If I were to ask just about anyone who walked into my gun shop why he or she wanted to buy a handgun, I would get the exact, same answer that I received from the guy who walked in one afternoon just before I went to conduct an interview at the youth jail. And when I asked those jail kids the same two questions, the responses would be also the same as how a customer would respond if asked him those questions in my shop.

So here we have two groups, one group comprised of the most law-abiding and well-behaved individuals in society, otherwise they wouldn't be able to purchase a legal gun. The other group was comprised of the most violent and most criminally minded in our society. Yet when it comes to the reason these individuals want to own the kind of gun which figures in most, if not almost all the 125,000 intentional gun injuries which occur every year in the United States, everyone in these two groups is saying exactly the same thing.

The purpose of this book is to explain how and why the rationales advanced for more versus less gun access are formed and how they are used to bolster their own arguments as well as to reject the arguments made by the other side. What you will learn is that the views and understanding about guns amongst the population which owns guns is no more based on reality than the views and understanding about guns held by individuals who would rather see America become a gun-free zone.

At 8 A.M. on Friday, December 12, 2012, a 20-year-old named Adam Lanza shot his way into the elementary school in Newtown, CT and within 4 minutes shot and killed 6 adults and 20 first-grade students.[2] Before driving to the school, Lanza shot and killed his mother Nancy while she slept in her bed. When he finished the rampage in the school from which he had graduated nine years previously, he took his own life with a bullet through his head.

Because Newtown is located less than one hour's drive from New York City, this event precipitated a media invasion and frenzy which prompted a national argument about the role of guns in American society which is still taking place.

Five years before the Newtown massacre, on April 16, 2007, a student at Virginia Tech University barricaded himself inside a campus building and by the time the cops were able to break through the doors, which was when the shooter, Seung Hui-Cho, shot himself to death, the carnage had resulted in the deaths of 32 students, faculty and staff and non-fatal injuries to 17 other students and school staff.[3]

Five years after the Newtown event, a man opened a window in the Mandalay Bay Hotel in Las Vegas on October 1, 2017, began shooting down at the crowd which had gathered for a music festival, and before he shot himself as security guards were breaking down his hotel room door, he killed 60 people and wounded 411 more.[4]

Over the entire decade beginning with the Virginia Tech massacre and ending with the mass shooting at the Mandalay Bay, more than 3,000 were killed and wounded in the 99 gun slaughters which the FBI defines as 'mass shootings,' the definition applied to any outbreak of gun violence in which at least 4 people are killed by a single individual in a public space.

This definition does not include shootings that occur in private properties, such as domestic and family violence that usually takes place in the home. It also is only applied to events in which 4 people are killed, not if 4 victims are both wounded and/or killed. If we were to change the definition of mass shootings to embrace every episode in which 4 individuals are shot even if none of them die, the number of such events would be at least twice as great as the number of mass shootings which result in at least 4 persons shot to death.

The 2012 mass shooting at the Newtown-Sandy Hook Elementary School was hardly the worst episode involving someone using a gun to kill and injure multiple victims in a public space. But what made the Sandy Hook episode different from previous or subsequent mass violence events, was that for the first time, a widespread and continuous argument about guns and the place of guns in American society broke out.

When two high school students ran through their school in Columbine, CO in 1999, and left 13 dead and 25 wounded before their spree ended, Bill Clinton then delivered a brief speech. In his remarks, he said the usual things about stopping people from using guns to commit such evil deeds and made a point of talking about how school children needed to be watched more carefully if they appeared to be depressed or otherwise unable to function in a normal way. Two weeks after the massacre, the NRA held its annual meeting in a convention center located 20 miles away from Columbine, and despite a few, minor protests, the meeting went off as scheduled.

Leaving aside whether the data on mass shootings or the data on gun violence in general can be exactly compared between the United States and other advanced (OECD) nation-states, there is no question that what is a rare or certainly infrequent event in other countries occurs on a relatively frequent and common basis in the United States.[5] The numbers which are usually presented show that the United States represents roughly 6% of the entire global population but suffers from more than 30% of worldwide mass shooting events.

This breakdown between privately-owned guns and mass shootings holds true for the comparison of population versus guns in private hands throughout the world as well because it's also the case that American households contain at least 30% of all privately-owned guns in the world today. If anything, the percentage of the worldwide private arsenal sitting in American households is probably substantially understated because many American gun manufacturers have gone out of business even though their guns are still lying around.[6] Hence, we can't get bottom-line data on the total number of all guns.

As inexact as the numbers may be, the number of mass shootings and the size of the privately-owned gun stock in America was never an issue for sustained discussion or public argument to any degree until the December 12, 2012, shootings at the Sandy Hook Elementary School. The lack of public debate about the presence and/or use of guns in American life prior to that date reflected the degree to which the National Rifle Association (NRA) represented one side of the issue, whereas there was no organized, grass-roots effort representing the other side.

Several weeks following the Sandy Hook shooting, however, the rhetorical and organizational gun-violence landscape began to change. This was because an internet marketing professional and temporary stay-at-home mom named Shannon Watts began promoting the idea of gun control on Facebook from her kitchen table in Indianapolis and very quickly shattered the monopoly about gun rhetoric that the NRA had enjoyed up to that point.

The group founded by Shannon Watts, *Moms Demand Action for Gun Sense* got some headlines and a bit of media notice over the next several years, but what Shannon really earned for all her efforts was that by 2014 she was flat broke. What saved her was a decision by the former Mayor of New York City, Mike Bloomberg, to invest $40 million a year in gun-control activities, most of which ended up being pledged to Shannon's group. As a result, her work took off.

For the first time since the NRA started operating back in 1871, the gun 'rights' organization, or as they preferred to call themselves, 'America's first civil rights' organization, found itself competing for media attention and political influence on multiple fronts. Not only did Bloomberg's money give Shannon Watts a necessary and potent lift, but operating through an umbrella organization, *Everytown for Gun Safety*, funds to support various gun-control initiatives began to spring up all over the place.

In particular, Everytown and its shrewd CEO, John Feinblatt, began looking at Congressional races where a candidate who supported gun-control legislation might replace someone whose votes on guns followed the way the NRA told him or her to vote. Money for 'gun sense' candidates not only went to men and women running for public office at the national level, but funds also went to state-legislative candidates because most gun laws are written in state legislatures and signed or not signed by the Governors of those states. In 2018, financial support for federal and state races went to more than 1,000 candidates.

At the same time that a true, grass-roots, gun-control movement was rearing its head, the NRA was shifting its organizational and rhetorical perspective in ways that would ultimately hurt the organization and render it much less effective in its promotion of gun 'rights.' Beginning in 2016, and no doubt partially in response to the growth of Everytown, MOMS and other gun-control groups, the NRA made three tactical decisions that would quickly undo much of the organization's control over the public discussion about guns up to that point.

The first decision was to jump into bed, politically speaking, with a Republican Presidential candidate named Donald Trump. The first time the NRA ever endorsed any Presidential candidate was after Ronald Reagan showed up at the 1980 NRA national show in Philadelphia, but the endorsement wasn't announced until just several weeks before the November vote. A late-breaking Presidential endorsement remained standard operating procedure for the NRA until 2016, when the organization showcased and then endorsed Trump on May 20, 2016, at their annual meet.

Trump had gone out of his way to promote himself as a 'champion' of gun 'rights,' including a comment in January, 2016 about how his supporters were so loyal, they would vote for him even if he shot someone dead in the street.[7] This inflammatory, pro-gun rhetoric was part and parcel of every campaign speech made by Trump, including multiple promises to maintain and strengthen 2nd-Amendment protections, as well as angry denunciations about how Democrats and liberals were against guns.

What may have also motivated the NRA to make unprecedented financial investments in the Trump campaign was the fear that if Hillary Clinton won the general election, which polls showed would probably be the case, that she would resurrect and pass the gun-control law that was developed in 1998 by the then-Secretary of HEW – Andrew Cuomo – which if enacted, would have probably ended the retail gun business in the United States.[8]

The problem, however, with buying into the Trump campaign in such an energetic and financially significant way was that this strategy also required the NRA to buy into an increasingly radical political posture which was advanced through the development of what turned out to be a mess known as NRA-TV.

The development of video outreach to replace what had always been a reliance on the printed word was the brainchild of the NRA's long-time advertising partner, Ackerman-McQueen. But the video feeds, in addition to being extremely far to the radical Right, were also just boring to the point that the audience numbers were never even close to what they were supposed to be. Ultimately, the NRA sued its advertiser, then fought a very public and nasty battle with its organizational President, Oliver North, who was also being paid by Ackerman-McQueen.

The shift towards a more aggressive political stance and the public arguments between Oliver North and the long-time Executive Vice President, Wayne LaPierre, cost the NRA both members and revenues, but the real threat to the organization came from a third decision, which was a basic shift in how the organization conducted its most important activity, namely, the gun-training program, which is what had been the original rationale for the development and original growth of the organization itself.

The NRA was founded in 1871 by two former veterans of the Civil War who felt that the war might have been won more quickly and at less human cost for the Union had the Federal army been better trained. In particular, the original NRA leadership felt that Americans needed to be more proficient in their use of small arms and thus a civilian organization devoted to gun proficiency was born.

At the time, the NRA first encountered a serious organizational challenge from gun-control groups, the first line of gun 'rights' defense was the 100,000+ certified NRA gun trainers who conducted as many as several million public training sessions every year. Many of these training events were held in states which required such training in order to purchase or carry around a gun; many other training activities took place in shooting ranges and other public venues which promoted the ownership and/or use of guns.

The NRA training programs were always conducted on a face-to-face basis and NRA trainers were encouraged and were often financially rewarded for using these sessions to promote the NRA and get new members to join. However, beginning in the 1970's and then becoming much more frequent in the following decade, many states began to issue concealed-carry gun licenses (CCW) and gun training became something of a cottage industry that grew up outside of the control and purview of the NRA.

In particular, the internet spawned a whole new approach to gun training based on video and digital gun training aids, and training groups like the United States Concealed Carry Association began to appear and challenge the NRA's training dominance as well as promoting shooting-related products like shooter's insurance which appealed to men and women who wanted to protect themselves with their guns.

The NRA's decision to abandon its traditional reliance on face-to-face training activities and sell an insurance product called Carry Guard turned out to be a disaster both in terms of the negative reaction of its training corps as well as the legal problems which arose from selling an insurance product that actually violated insurance laws and regulations in many states.

Taken together, these three issues – aggressive, alt-right politics, lawsuits back and forth between NRA and Ackerman-McQueen, missteps in the training division – all made it easier for gun-control organizations like Everytown and MOMS to begin challenging the NRA in the public media arena and make up for more than a century of lost time.[9]

When Wayne LaPierre went on television and gave a fiery, no-compromise defense of guns a week after the 2012 massacre at Sandy Hook, there was little response from the gun-control crowd. But after a young man invaded the high school in Parkland Florida and killed 17 people in 2018, the media's coverage was dominated by statements from individuals and groups calling for more gun control, and a national tour led by several of the Parkland students who survived the attack made more than 50 stops around the country over the following six months.

As this text is being prepared for final production, at the end of June 2022, President Joe Biden has just signed the fifth federal gun law in response to a massacre at an elementary school in Texas which killed 19 students and 2 teachers while law enforcement stayed outside the school for nearly an hour while the rampage went on.

The new gun bill, however, makes very few alterations to federal regulations covering guns, covering a slight expansion of the background check process for persons under 21 years of age and closing a loophole which could let persons committing certain kinds of domestic assaults to clear a background check. The new law also appropriates funding to be directed towards mental health counseling and violence intervention activities conducted by neighborhood groups and creates a specific 'gun trafficking' offense to be listed in federal criminal law.

Although the 2022 law has been the first federal gun-control law passed since the Brady bill was enacted in 1994, the number of state-level gun-control statutes enacted since Sandy Hook is three times as many as laws which make it easier to purchase, own or walk around with a gun. In particular, background checks for private gun transfers have been passed in 13 states, along with 19 'red flag' laws which create a process for temporary or permanent removal of a gun owner's guns. The 2022 law does not contain either a comprehensive background check provision, or any mention of 'red flag' procedures, both being eliminated in order to secure necessary GOP votes.

The pro-gun movement has also been active in pushing laws which liberalize how guns are purchased and used, focusing most of their attention on allowing individuals to carry a concealed weapon without requiring a special permit to walk around armed. In fact, there are now 17 states that have passed what is referred to as 'Constitutional carry,' the idea being that passing a background check to purchase a gun is the only legal requirement standing in the way of carrying a concealed gun outside the home.

The day before Biden signed the gun bill into law, the Supreme Court issued a ruling which effectively overturned a New York State law which requires the issuance of carry-concealed licenses to be based on the applicant demonstrating a specific 'need' to carry a gun outside of the home. New York was one of 6 states which gave law enforcement wide latitude in deciding legal authority for concealed-carry (CCW) which means the other 'may issue' states will no doubt become 'shall-issue' CCW states as well.

The advocacy by organizations promoting more versus less government intervention over gun ownership is what has created the ongoing debate about guns, gun rights and gun violence which only flared up occasionally prior to Sandy Hook. But it isn't just the occasional, spectacular mass shootings which now provoke outbreaks of the gun debate. As pointed out above, the number of privately-owned guns, their use in criminal attacks and their use as protections from such arracks are also unique features of American life, and all three elements contribute to, and shape the ongoing debate about guns.

This book will examine the key issues which form the content and context of the argument about guns, and will explain how individuals who own guns, along with the population which doesn't own guns, both create as well as believe gun narratives which have little, if any basis in truth or facts. Which is why both sides in the gun debate get the argument wrong a lot more than they get it right. The issues we will examine are:

- Do guns protect us or harm us, i.e., are guns a positive or negative factor when it comes to community safety and community peace?
- What kind and how much training should individuals need to undergo if they want to own and use guns?
- Does the ATF play a positive or negative role in regulating the ownership and use of guns?
- Do we understand how social factors like socio-economic-status and race impact the violence connected to the use of guns?
- Should gun violence be considered a public health problem?
- Is the 2nd Amendment a carte-blanche for owning guns?
- How can we prevent mass shootings?

- Is there a gun 'culture and is there an anti-gun culture?

We will devote a chapter to each of these issues and then offer a wholly different approach to what, if anything, we should do about guns, gun ownership and gun violence in the United States. Our solution will be based primarily on the fact that I have been engaged in the gun business, one way or another, for nearly 60 years. At various times I have been connected to guns as a consumer, gun dealer, gun wholesaler, gun importer, gun manufacturer and certified gun trainer, all of which gives me a rather unique perspective on America and its guns.

What brings me to the gun issue from a different and unparalleled point of view is that I do not embellish the research and the data by holding an occasional discussion with several individuals from the groups whose existence and activity creates the debate over why Americans love their guns. In fact, over the years I have probably talked in detail to hundreds of gun owners, as well as to countless individuals who belong to gun-control organizations in front of whom I have appeared and spoken God knows how many times.

This book cites all the necessary and relevant research done on guns both in terms of benefits and risks. But this information cannot explain how come there are 100 million Americans like me who first started playing around with guns when they were kids but feel better if at least some of their guns are still around.

How do we make such individuals understand that it's not the gun which is the problem, but the way certain types of guns are used more than 100 times every day?

Chapter 1

Do We Need Guns?

The Federal Government got into the gun business before there was a Federal Government when a group of colonial patriots in 1777 started manufacturing rifles for the colonial army at a facility alongside the Connecticut River in Springfield, MA. From the beginnings of settlement in New England, the Connecticut River Valley had been the location for many manufacturing operations which produced the metal parts for small arms, to the point that the area was also referred to as Gun Valley and was therefore a natural choice for the development of a government-run facility to produce weapons of war.[10]

In 1789, President George Washington convinced Congress to appropriate funds to expand and modernize the arsenal, his decision to locate it permanently in Springfield allegedly based on the shallowness of the Connecticut River at that point which prevented the British from bringing heavy gunships above Hartford to demolish the gun factory with bombardments from heavy naval guns. The real story was that Washington's decision to locate the arsenal in Massachusetts was a payoff to his friend Henry Knox, whose remarkable overland shipment of cannons from Ticonderoga to Boston broke the British siege and probably kept the Revolutionary War alive in 1776.

The United States continued to build military arms at Springfield but did not pass a national gun law until 1934, when a spate of criminal violence tied to organized crime and prohibition (e.g., Al Capone and the 1929 St. Valentine's Day massacre) brought about legislation that made the process of owning a fully-automatic weapon much more difficult than purchasing or owning a semi-automatic gun.

As long as a gun could only fire one bullet each time the trigger was pulled, as opposed to discharging multiple rounds with one trigger pull, any adult who claimed to be a law-abiding citizen could purchase a semi-automatic handgun in the state where he/she lived, but semi-automatic long guns could be shipped from a manufacturer or a dealer to a customer across a state line or multiple state lines. The bolt-action rifle which Oswald used to kill President Kennedy and wounded Governor Connally in 1963 was mailed to Oswald in Texas from a sporting-goods warehouse in Illinois.

The national government got into regulating gun ownership big-time with the Gun Control Act (GCA68) passed in 1968. This statute was first introduced after Kennedy's assassination and became the template for all federal gun regulatory activity from then until now. The law had three major provisions: First, it made the Alcohol, Tobacco, Firearms (and Explosives) Division of the Treasury Department responsible for regulating gun commerce between the states, with all interstate gun shipments only allowed to go between federally-licensed gun dealers whose way of doing business had been defined by the second gun law passed by the Roosevelt Administration in 1938.

Second, GCA68 defined the term 'law-abiding' by creating a procedure whereby anyone purchasing or receiving a gun from a federally-licensed dealer not only had to provide proof of age and residence in the same state where the dealer was located, but also had to affirm that he/she did not have a history of certain behaviors that disqualified the individual from possessing a gun. These prohibitions against gun ownership included having been charged with a felony, being a fugitive from justice, having been adjudicated as mentally ill or addicted to alcohol or drugs or having received a less than honorable discharge from the military.

Third, GCA68 prohibited the import of cheaply-made foreign guns that were small and easily concealable, but also could be sold for a minimum price and therefore find their way into the 'wrong' hands. In fact, this provision of GCA68 was really an effort to protect domestic gun makers from cheap, foreign goods, but it also fostered the impression that only law-abiding Americans would be willing to spend additional dollars for guns that were better made.[11]

It should be noted that even though it is often presumed that manufacturing techniques developed at the Springfield Arsenal – assembly-line movements, interchangeable parts – became the basic manufacturing model for the entire Industrial Revolution, in fact small arms had first been designed and manufactured in Europe by gun companies like Beretta in Italy or Stopler in Germany from the 16th Century on.

What made the American gun market attractive to gun manufacturers from overseas, however, was not the potential for selling cheaply-made small arms, but the fact that the United States was the only country which developed a regulatory environment for guns that focused not on the gun design so much as on the behavior of individuals who wanted to own guns. Other than the distinction between full-automatic and semi-automatic weapons, GCA68 did not prohibit the sale of any type of gun, as long as it required a separate trigger pull to fire each round.

In fact, even with GCA68 on the books, Americans could still purchase and own fully-automatic guns like the Thompson submachine gun which became something of a cultural icon after it was used in the St. Valentine's Day massacre and was also favored by such Prohibition-era gangsters as Machine Gun Kelly and Pretty Boy Floyd.

The gun is still manufactured and sold as a semi-automatic weapon, and it looks like this:

Figure 1. Thompson semi-automatic gun.

If you want to pretend that you're Machine Gun Kelly, you can also purchase one of those round magazines which holds 100 cartridges of 45-caliber ammunition, but it will cost an additional $600 beyond the cost of the gun, which usually retails for around $2,000 in semi-auto mode. The full-auto gun, which is prized by collectors, may set someone back as much as $10,000, if and when a model comes up for sale.

From a licensing point of view, obtaining the original submachine gun is covered by the procedures found in the first federal gun law, the NFA34. If a gun is on the NFA34 restricted list, a would-be owner must first pay $250 for a special treasury stamp, then undergo a more detailed background check conducted by both the local cops and the feds. The whole paperwork deal can take up to six months, but if you're willing to be patients and wait, sooner or later you'll have your gun.

There are somewhere around 60,000 machine guns or submachine guns in private American hands. The last time that one of these weapons was used in a criminal assault was 1947 or maybe 1948. GCA68 did not outlaw the ownership of such weapons, it just recognized that these guns were too dangerous to be sold quickly and easily over the counter at the local gun shop. Which is why such weapons almost never show up in violent crimes.

Unfortunately, the more stringent regulatory procedure covering full-automatic weapons in NFA34 didn't carry over to how semi-automatic weapons are regulated either through NFA34 or GCA68. In particular, GCA68 created an entire regulatory environment for guns based on the behavior and personal histories of potential or actual gun owners while the issue of gun lethality based on gun design was and still remains entirely outside the purview of federal gun laws.

When other advanced countries like Germany and France adopted gun regulations before and after World War II, they copied the NFA34 statute except that semi-automatic handguns were also listed as requiring strict licensing procedures so as to limit the number and availability of such weapons in civilian hands. But the difference between the relatively lax procedures applied to the ownership of handguns and semi-automatic rifles by NFA34 and the stricter licensing requirements imposed for such weapons in other advanced countries is not, as is usually explained, because of the 2nd Amendment's injunction allowing for Americans to 'keep and bear arms.'

The preambles to NFA34 and GCA68 explain and justify these gun regulations as a response to crime and as a means for making it easier for law enforcement to deal with crime. On the other hand, in Western countries which copied NFA34, the rationale was stated as governments wanting to keep dangerous weapons out of the hands of radicals and revolutionaries whose behavior, particularly mass strikes and other forms of organized strife, could become a threat to the power and authority of the national state.

Virtually every Western country other than the United States experienced significant mass violence and radical protests before and after World War I and then again before World War II. America was the only industrialized nation that did not become embroiled in the kind of mass and incessant street violence that occurred just about everywhere else, nor did mass political challenges from the Right or the Left ever emerge and become commonplace or continuous in the United States. However, in Germany, France, Italy and even England, pitched battles between Right and Left political parties as well as serious and sustained labor uprisings were more common than not, and were certainly a major factor in the collapse of parliamentary governments throughout the West.

While strikes and other labor-induced violence also took place in the United States during the late 19th Century and the first several decades of the 20th Century (ex. the 1886 Haymarket bombing) at no time was the existence or authority of the federal government ever threatened, nor was police power in any jurisdiction the target of mass violence or even widespread criminal attacks. In this respect, with the exception of the Civil War, the United States was always the most law-abiding society in the Western, industrial world, which was a major factor contributing to the continued growth of our civilian arsenal based on the idea that any law-abiding individual could buy and own a gun.

The benevolent attitude of the national government towards private gun ownership began to change, however, with the advent of the Clinton Administration in 1994. The shift towards a more restrictive legal environment for gun owners came about largely because of a near-quadrupling of the violent crime rate from 160 violent crimes per 100,000 people in the early 1960's, to 750 crimes per 100,000 people in the early 1990's, an increase driven by a doubling of the murder rate and a quintupling(!) of the aggravated assault rate, both crimes often committed with guns.

The Clinton Administration made two major initiatives in the federal approach to gun ownership. It strengthened the focus on the behavior of individuals who wanted to become gun owners by passing the Brady Bill in 1993, which required that all transfers of guns between federally-licensed dealers and prospective customers be preceded with a background check for disqualifying behavior conducted by the FBI. This procedure replaced what had been an 'honor system' process whereby the prospective gun owner had to assert that he/she had not been convicted of a felony or otherwise been engaged in a disqualifying type of behavior, but no validation of this pre-purchase claim was performed.

The second Clinton gun-control initiative known as the assault weapons ban, was passed in 1994 as part of a federal crime bill, and it marked a major shift in how the federal government would define and enforce gun control. For the first time since NFA34, this law focused not on the behavior and background of gun owners, but on the lethality of certain kinds of gun designs.

In particular, the law banned certain semi-auto rifles which could take bottom-loading, high-capacity magazines, as well as other features found on military-style guns. Handgun magazines which held more than 10 rounds were also banned but both existing assault rifles and high-capacity magazines owned by civilians were grandfathered in and did not need to be turned in or relinquished from current ownership. The law was vigorously fought by the gun industry and the ensuing debate unleashed the basic narratives that formed the arguments about guns on both sides, arguments that were backed up by serious research.

Neither side tried to deny the lethality and dangerousness of guns as consumer products, but both sides attempted to create a context in which gun risk was seen as a positive or a negative issue depending on how and in what context the gun was used. The argument which presented the lethality of guns as a positive feature was made first and most powerfully by Gary Kleck, a criminologist at Florida State University, whose team conducted telephone interviews with slightly less than 5,000 respondents, and extrapolating from these discussions, Kleck estimated that what he called defensive gun use (DGU) – brandishing, showing, shooting – occurred as often as 2 million times every year.[12]

Unfortunately, when Kleck's interviewers went into specific details with respondents about what actually happened during the incident where a gun was allegedly used to prevent a threat from taking place, complete data could only be gathered from slightly more than 200 individuals, of whom two-thirds claimed they had made some mention of the incident to the police. On the other hand, less than 10% of the specific DGU events occurred in a public space, as opposed to nearly 80% taking place in or nearby the defender's home.

At best, Kleck's evidence created a rather ambiguous picture of the value of guns for self-defense against threats or actual assaults. The biggest problem was that respondents who claimed they protected themselves with a DGU, were not asked whether the same outcome would have been achieved if they had responded to the threatened or actual attack in a different way. What would have happened, for example, if an individual defending himself or herself yelled at the attacker and threatened to call the police? Would the outcome of such events have been different or the same?

Kleck's global study, again extrapolating the actual numbers, found that as many as 400,000 people believe they saved a life because they responded to an attack or the threat of an attack by using a gun which made the life-saving value of gun use go far beyond the numbers of people who lose their lives each year through the use of guns.

It was this statistic which more than any other issue raised by Kleck that immediately turned this paper into the basic narrative used by the gun industry to justify civilian ownership of guns specifically designed and sold for self-protection and response to actual or perceived criminal threats. If anything, losing 15,000 lives a year to gun violence was a small price to pay for guns being used to save 400,000 lives.

Kleck published his research in 1995, several years after two physicians and public health researchers – Arthur Kellerman and Frederick Rivara – published two research papers in a medical journal which found that access to a gun in the home created a risk for homicide and suicide.[13] The homicide study was based on interviews with 420 individuals who served as proxies for victims of homicides, of which 209 victims were shot and killed with guns. These interviews found a substantially-higher rate of homicide in homes which contained a gun, with the use of illicit drugs and a history of physical fights also being found to be risks.

A heightened risk of suicide in homes with guns was also found in a similar study covering 554 cases of suicide, of which 326 victims killed themselves by using guns. As in their study of gun homicides, the Kellerman and Rivara team interviewed individuals who served as proxies for the victims and in both studies, a case-control method was used to compare victims to non-victims based on similar socio-economic demographics.

Just as Gary Kleck's study was used and continues to be used by the gun industry to push back against more stringent gun controls, so the research published by Kellerman and Rivara was cited by the gun-control community, particularly because the articles appeared when Clinton's gun bills were in the process of being debated and eventually passed.

The publication of the Kellerman-Rivara research, however, would bring about a major shift in the scope of government-funded gun research insofar as the two articles had received financial support from the CDC. This created a backlash leading to the curtailment of CDC gun research funding in 1997, a hiatus which lasted until 2021.

On the other hand, the disappearance of government financial support did not foreclose other funding options, in particular support from private sources like the Joyce Foundation which delivered $32 million in research grants between 1993 and 2018. One of the recipients of Joyce support has been David Hemenway, who runs the Injury Control Research Center at Harvard University's School of Public Health. His work is responsible for the development of a narrative on gun violence which has become the basic argument of the gun-control movement over the past several decades.

Hemenway and his colleagues have published multiple studies comparing fatal criminal activity and gun ownership in advanced (OECD) countries and what their research shows is that while violent crime rates do not differ significantly between the United States and other OECD countries, fatal violence rates are 7 to 20 times higher in the United States than anywhere else.[14] Comparing various social and economic factors between countries, a regression analysis pinpoints access to guns as the primary factor in America's high fatal violence rate.

Hemenway's explanation for fatal violence has been adopted by the entire gun-control community and the causal connection between the size of our civilian arsenal and the heightened level of fatal violence is a cornerstone of the narrative used by every organization that promotes stricter controls over the ownership and use of guns.

Unfortunately, the data utilized by Hemenway and his research colleagues to make the argument about more guns equals more gun violence happens not to be evidence that Hemenway and others should be using for this proposition for the simple reason that there is no relationship between how *many* guns are in private hands and what *types* of guns are used to commit violent crimes.

In an analysis of more than 840,000 crime guns inventoried by more than one thousand police agencies in 36 states and the District of Columbia between 2010 and 2016, less than 5% of these guns were manufactured by companies that make and sell most of the guns used for hunting and sport shooting throughout the United States: Remington, Winchester, Mossberg, Marlin, and Savage Arms.

This national inventory of guns sitting in police department storage facilities did not, however, contain information on the specific models and types of guns, and gun companies which manufactured long guns – rifles and shotguns – also made handguns from time to time. But we were able to analyze the pattern of crime guns very specifically from another set of data which was a listing of 7,926 guns confiscated in 2014 by police departments in Chicago, Baltimore, and St. Louis, which happened to be major locations for crime violence not just in 2014 but every year.[15]

Of the crime guns confiscated in these three cities, 70% were center-fire handguns, of which half were manufactured by Smith & Wesson, Taurus, Glock, Ruger, Beretta, Colt, and Springfield Arms. Of the other 2,300 handguns, more than half were cheap, junk guns which we used to call 'Saturday night specials,' with more than 1,000 of these guns being at least 30 years old.

In other words, when we use a generic term like 'guns' to talk about gun violence or to compare gun violence between the United States and the rest of the OECD, the comparison falls apart simply because no other advanced country gives its residents free access to handguns the way residents can purchase and move handguns from person to person in the United States.

We are not trying or intending to discount the connection between our country's elevated fatal violence rate and the size of our civilian arsenal. But if we were to take Hemenway's regression analyses and connect gun-violence metrics to the number of guns which *cause* that violence, we would have results that are more realistic about guns and violence than the results we now have now which are used to create the basic narrative both about gun violence and gun control.

For the same reason, the argument on the other side about how guns make us safe and actually reduce gun violence events, is just as devoid of reality as what has been promoted by Hemenway and his research colleagues and organizational peers.

In particular, the narrative which links gun ownership to more, rather than less physical safety and reduced criminality can be found in the book, *More Guns, Less Crime*, first published by an economist, John Lott, in 1998.[16] This book appeared at the same time that state laws which made it easier to obtain permission to carry a concealed weapon were beginning to appear following the passage of such a law in Florida in 1978.

Prior to the Florida statute, most states required a detailed explanation usually tied to a business activity, in order to justify carrying concealed weapons outside the home. Florida's law removed those restrictions and made concealed-carry contingent only on a background check which would not turn up any of the disqualifying legal issues for gun ownership as defined in GCA68.

The issuance of concealed-carry licenses being tied only to a law-abiding personal history became known as 'shall issue,' as opposed to the 'may issue' procedure which still required the issuing authority (usually the police) to make a determination of someone's legal fitness to walk around the neighborhood with a concealed gun.

Lott's book was based on a comparison of the issuance of 'shall issue' concealed-carry permits with crime rates in the same jurisdictions and what he found was that, generally speaking, as the issuance of concealed-carry permits increased, so the rate of serious crime decreased. He argued that the decrease in crime was due to the realization on the part of the would-be attacker that his potential victim might now be armed.

The problem with Lott's approach, however, is that while fatal and non-fatal physical assaults went down in jurisdictions that began issuing concealed-carry permits, the number and rate of impersonal crime of stealth (burglary) went up. And here is where Lott's work and his attempt to explain the shift from personal to impersonal criminal events begins to fall apart.

In arguing that criminals make a conscious decision to change their criminal behavior based on the possibility that their victim might be armed and thus pose a greater risk to the attacker, Lott is assuming that the same population is engaged in two very different types of criminality and switches from one category of criminal behavior to another based on rational, planned belief and thought.

If we know one thing about physical assaults, particularly assaults which result in a fatality, most such events are not planned on any rational, thoughtful basis at all. Physical assaults usually occur between individuals who know each, have been engaged in some kind of dispute which is ongoing and is frequently seen by both parties as being beyond repair.

Burglary, on the other hand, is based on observation, careful planning, and an awareness that the property which is stolen will have some value when sold to someone else. In other words, not only are physical assaults and impersonal crimes of stealth committed in very different ways, but they are usually also committed by a different group of individuals, rather than the same person deciding that he will commit one type of crime instead of another type of crime.

The problem with Hemenway's research which argues that guns are a risk versus Lott's research which promotes the idea that guns are a benefit, is that both arguments find a coincidence in how separate trends change at the same time, but coincidence is not causality and the explanations offered by both scholars ad their followers about the causal connection between more crime or less crime versus more guns or less guns are conclusions in search of supporting evidence rather than the other way around.

Hemenway and other public health scholars who focus on gun violence as a health problem have spilled gallons of ink criticizing how Lott uses regression methodologies which they believe are not valid statistical approaches to the issue of whether guns are a good thing or a bad thing when it comes to the elevated rate of gun violence in the United States. Yet such criticisms entirely miss the point about Lott's assumption that the same people who commit violent assaults then turn around and commit burglaries when the possible assault victim may turn out to be armed.

The critics of Lott's research also miss a second, important point about the use of concealed-carry license issuances as a method to determine how many individuals are walking around armed. Let me give you a personal experience which sheds an interesting perspective on the reasons why using such data to say anything about how and why there has been an increase in concealed-carry licensing must be managed with extreme care.

York County is a beautiful, farming area lying about 50 miles due west of Philadelphia and is easily reachable by driving through the Pennsylvania Dutch Country on picturesque U.S. Route 30. In the middle of the county is the town of York which is the county seat.

York has a very nice gun show several times each year with many of the tables rented by local guys who want to sell or trade some old gun-related junk and lots of other tables selling home-made food, jewelry, and other knick-knacks. In other words, the show is basically a big garage sale and while generally speaking it's a law-abiding crowd, the local cops and the ATF agents don't seem all that concerned about making sure that the paperwork is totally and completely under control.

One year I was at the show and the legislature had just made a change in the concealed-carry law making it easier to get a permit to walk around with a gun. Pennsylvania has been a 'shall issue' state since 1988, which means that anyone who can pass a background check can qualify to carry a concealed gun outside their home. But the year I was at the York gun show, some legal change had just been put into effect for concealed-carry, and the York County Sheriff was so overwhelmed by the number of people who lined up at his office that he had to hire some additional part-time help.

The story about the long line at the York County Sheriff had gotten back to Philadelphia, and the day of the gun show two reporters from Philadelphia newspapers showed up to find out what was going on. I happened to overhear the conversation between these two reporters and a couple of guys who had just come back from the Sheriff's office after waiting several hours in line.

The interview between the reporters and these two York residents, typical gun guys in their 50's, went like this:

Reporter: What was so important that you were willing to stand on a three-hour line?

Gun guy: Oh, I'm not going to be without a license. I want to carry my gun.

Reporter: What's so important about being able to carry a gun?

Gun guy: Gotta protect myself. Crime is getting really bad around here.

Reporter: Are you aware that there hasn't been a serious felony committed in York in the last three years?

Gun guy: That may be true. But *they* can always drive out here from Philadelphia.

Note the 'they.' The population which commits violent crimes, particularly assaults, is overwhelmingly a population which could never purchase or own a legal firearm because most of them could never pass a background check. People (and they are overwhelmingly males) who are charged with violent felonies didn't lead nice, lawful lives and then all of a sudden became violent criminals in their 20's or beyond. The research is very clear on this point: violent offenders have been committing serious and violent crimes long before they are old enough to walk into a gun shop and purchase a gun.

This same profile happens to fit most of the victims of violent crimes, particularly homicides and aggravated assaults. In fact, research shows that in as many as half of all homicides, the behavior that precipitated the fatal assault was committed by the victim of the attack.

It may be the case that would-be aggressors who decide to use a gun in a violent attack against someone else would caution their behavior based on the possibility that their victim might also be armed. But such a mental construct based on the issuance of concealed-carry licenses isn't tenable for the simple reason that residents of neighborhoods where most street violence occurs ate infrequent recipients of licenses which would allow them to carry guns. Indeed, John Lott himself has published work on the refusal or reluctance of licensing authorities to take an even-handed approach to issuing gun licenses to inner-city residents, particularly such residents who are people of color.

On the other hand, if scholars like John Lott, whose research promotes gun ownership as a positive end, confuse gun licensing with gun access, so scholars like David Hemenway, whose research is conducted to show the negatives of guns, also confuse gun ownership with gun violence for the simple reason noted above, namely by focusing their concern on the large number of privately-owned guns which are types and models which are rarely, if ever used in assaults with guns.

Neither Hemenway nor any other scholar who promotes the idea that more guns mean more, not less violent crime, has ever attempted to compare gun ownership based on types of guns and violent crime rates between the United States and the rest of the OECD because no other country breaks down data on gun ownership between guns that are used in violent crime as opposed to guns that are used for hunting and other activities which have nothing to do with crime.

Earlier in this chapter I presented some data about the types of guns that were picked up in felonies committed in three high-crime cities: Chicago, Baltimore ad St. Louis. Most of the guns were handguns, with half being products from major handgun manufacturers like Smith & Wesson, Beretta, and Glock. If these types of guns weren't available on the consumer market, if ownership of such weapons were restricted the way that access to such guns occurs in the rest of the OECD, would we have a fatal violence rate that is 7 to 20 times higher than in all the other advanced nation-states?

It can be said with some degree of certainty that the argument about the social utility of guns (i.e., guns are 'good,' or guns are 'bad') is the fundamental point of departure on which the entire debate between the two sides is based. Moreover, both sides make a point of insisting that their arguments are based on solid research. Unfortunately, the research happens to be wrong. Despite the plethora of data advanced by the 'more guns mean less crime' school versus the 'more guns mean more crime' school, in both instances the data has gaps which render both arguments moot.

If the population which is responsible for the perpetration and victimization of most violent crime are usually hard-core felons while still in their teens, why is the issuance of a license based on an unblemished legal history of any concern? For that matter, if fatal gun assaults are overwhelmingly committed with small, concealable handguns, who cares how many hunting rifles and shotguns are found in American homes?

What makes the 'good gun' versus 'bad gun' argument so far removed from reality is one basic fact, namely, that 80% of all intentional gun injuries – homicides, aggravated assaults – are also felonies, which means that public access to crime data is extremely limited., thus researchers cannot retrieve or use data which is essential for understanding how and why these violent events occur. Hence, both sides end up inventing their explanations as to why gun violence happens, as well as why the rate of such violence changes from time to time.

In 2019 a physician and public health researcher, Michael Siegel, published an article which looked at homicide and suicide rates in all 50 states over a twenty-five year period and compared the state-by-state number against the number of gun laws in each state.[17] This comparison, according to Siegel and his research colleagues, found that passage of two gun laws – universal background checks and violent misdemeanors – resulted in a significant decline in gun homicides.

To be more exact, the researchers didn't find a clear connection between more gun laws and less violent crime. The term which appears whenever a study is published which is based on regression methodology is that the two factors, more laws, and less crime, are 'associated' with each other, whatever that means.

What was the result of this study? Promoting universal background checks has become the *numero uno* legislative and strategic focus of every gun-control organization and group.

This study also found that the state with the highest rate of gun violence – Louisiana – had the least number of laws regulating guns on its books, whereas the state with one of the lowest gun-violence rates – Massachusetts – had the highest number of laws controlling the ownership and use of guns.

Note that this research focused on laws which cover how people behave with guns, which is the same approach utilized by John Lott and other pro-gun researchers. Indeed, Siegel and his colleagues made a point of saying that "changes in household gun ownership were not found to be significantly associated with homicide or suicide rates."

How did Siegel and his colleagues figure out how many guns were in gun-owning households? They used what is referred to as 'proxies' for this information, meaning data which may be generated by the existence of a gun in the home, such as gun licenses, hunting licenses, memberships in organizations which support gun ownership, and other behaviors typically associated with people who own and/or use guns. The attempt to figure out valid proxies for determining which households have guns and whether this number is increasing, or decreasing has spawned its own little cottage research industry over the years.

But what if a state doesn't have a state-licensing system? What if the individuals most likely to hold hunting licenses own hunting guns like rifles and shotguns but don't necessarily own handguns, which are the guns used in just about all intentional gun injuries and deaths? You end up by saying that your research shows an 'association' between gun laws and gun injuries, which is about the best you can do.

There is, however, one method that can be used to determine the relative degree of gun ownership from one state to another, which then can be used to better understand the 'association' between gun laws and gun violence or, for that matter, to figure out if there is any real connection between these two factors at all.

The hard data on gun ownership is available in the monthly reports issued by the FBI on how many background checks are performed by their NICS operators, and the reasons for these calls. By definition, someone who is the subject of a background check performed by FBI-NICS is a gun owner, and this individual's identity isn't important. What's important is that the moment the background check is performed and approved, another gun has been added to the privately-owned guns in that state.

Breaking down private gun ownership to a household level is a rather pointless exercise if someone is trying to figure out the connection between the existence of state gun laws and gun violence, because the laws apply to every state resident, and we can get good data on the number of fatal and non-fatal gun injuries which occur in every state.

That being said, let's take the data on state gun laws developed by Siegel, et al., and compare it to intentional gun deaths as published by the CDC. We will look at 2016 because this was the last year covered in Siegel's study which found an 'association' between more laws regulating gun ownership and less violent crime.

In 2016, according to Siegel, Louisiana had the highest rate of fatal gun violence and the least number of state-level gun laws. The overall gun-homicide rate was 14.2, the highest of all 50 states, and the only two gun laws on the books were laws that sanctioned not backing down when threatened or attacked ('stand your ground' laws) and a law which removed police from exercising any discretion over who could and could not own a gun ('shall issue' laws.)

At the other end of the scale, Massachusetts had the sixth-lowest gun-homicide rate of all 50 states and also had enacted 5 of the 7 gun-control laws on the books in 2016. The only laws regulating guns that had not been enacted in Massachusetts were the statutes prohibiting gun ownership by persons convicted of violent misdemeanors and prohibiting gun trafficking – Massachusetts being one of only five states with universal background checks prior to 1991.

In 2016, Louisiana residents purchased 171,588 handguns. The state population was 4.7 million. That same year, with a population of 6.7 million, Massachusetts residents bought 75,977 handguns. With a statewide population in Louisiana which was 60% of the statewide Massachusetts population, residents in Louisiana introduced more than twice as many handguns into the state's civilian arsenal than moved into private hands in the Bay State. Or to put it another way, the per-capita number of handguns which were added to private gun collections in Louisiana was three times as large as the additional, per-capita growth of handguns in Massachusetts.

How come the study by Siegel and other studies on the impact of gun-control laws on gun violence list all kinds of socio-economic-demographic characteristics of the population being studied (age, gender, race, income, etc.) but only fleetingly mention the issue of guns, if it is mentioned at all? How come the proponents of guns as preventing, rather than promoting crime, focus on the behavior of gun owners but also ignore the issue of guns?

For that matter, when Gary Kleck and his team asked several hundred respondents to describe in detail how they used a guns to protect themselves from an actual or possible criminal attack, not a single individual who allegedly used a gun in self-defense was asked to describe the gun. When John Lott compared trends of crime to trends of issuance of concealed-carry licenses, why did he assume that someone who now had the legal right to carry a gun was actually walking around with a gun?

The answer to all those questions on both sides of the gun debate is simply this: The individuals whose research and advocacy inform both sides in the gun debate share one, basic point of view, namely, none of them know very much about guns. And because they don't know very much about guns, when they ask gun owners about their guns, they never go beyond the most superficial and meaningless question: why do you own a gun?

Chapter 2

Does Training Make a Gun 'Safe?'

Every gun manufactured in the United States or imported for commercial sale from overseas, must be shipped to a gun dealer with a set of safety instructions and a gun lock. Here is the first page of the safety manual included with every handgun made by Sturm, Ruger & Co.:

INSTRUCTION
MANUAL
FOR

RUGER AMERICAN®
PISTOL
STANDARD MODEL

– Rugged, Reliable Firearms® –

READ THE INSTRUCTIONS AND
WARNINGS IN THIS MANUAL CAREFULLY
BEFORE USING THIS FIREARM

© 2021 Sturm, Ruger & Co., Inc.

This manual may not be reproduced in whole or in part without the express written permission of Sturm, Ruger & Co., Inc.

For Service on This Model Please Call:
(336) 949-5200 (See p. 36)

TH S NSTRUCT ON MANUA SHOU D A WAYS ACCOMPANY TH S F REARM AND BE TRANSFERRED W TH T UPON CHANGE OF OWNERSH P, OR WHEN THE F REARM S OANED OR PRESENTED TO ANOTHER PERSON

Ruger.com

Figure 2. Ruger safety manual.

The following 5 pages containing specific safety instructions from safety laws enacted in a dozen different states which must be included in the safety manual for the gun to be sold in those states, the safety instructions from Ruger then has the following page:

FIREARMS SAFETY IS YOUR RESPONSIBILITY

SAFETY MUST BE THE FIRST AND CONSTANT CONSIDERATION OF EVERY PERSON WHO HANDLES FIREARMS AND AMMUNITION.

This Instruction Manual is designed to assist you in learning how to use and care for your **RUGER AMERICAN® PISTOL** with manual safety properly. Please contact us if you have any questions.

Only when you are certain you fully understand the manual and can properly carry out its instructions should you practice loading, unloading, etc. with live ammunition. If you have any doubts about your ability to handle or use a particular type of firearm safely, you should seek supervised instruction. Such personalized instruction often is available from local firearm retailers, gun clubs or police departments. If none of these sources can help, visit nra.org or write to the following address:

National Rifle Association
11250 Waples Mill Road
Fairfax, VA 22030-7400

The person possessing a firearm has a full-time job. You cannot guess; you cannot forget. You must know how to use your firearm safely. Do not use any firearm without having a complete understanding of its particular characteristics and safe use. Remember: There is no such thing as a foolproof firearm.

Figure 3. Ruger safety instructions.

Note the manual makes no attempt to disguise or otherwise describe this consumer product as an item which can be handled or used without being concerned about safety. The same type of narrative is found in the safety instructions which accompany every Glock.

The issue of gun safety was never raised in any meaningful way until the gun-control movement began to sprout wings after Sandy Hook. Prior to that time, nobody in the gun business really paid attention to whether or not guns were safe or unsafe, because nobody had any reason to challenge the existence or presence of guns. After Sandy Hook, however, the gun-control movement made the dangerousness of guns yet another reason more gun control measures needed to be discussed, turned into legislative remedies, and passed into laws.

Figure 4. Glock safety manual.

But before we begin discussing the safety measures which gun-control advocates wanted to see on the books, we should look at some data to determine just exactly how much danger is represented by accidental injuries caused by guns. Here are the 2020 numbers for accidental deaths in the United States:

Total accidental deaths, all ages	200,955
Drug overdoses	83,558
Automobile accidents	42,339
Falls	42,114
Drowning	4,589
Home fires	2,564
Guns	535

Of the accidental gun deaths, the CDC reports that 93 were children up to the age of fourteen. Since most states grant hunting licenses beginning at age fifteen, we can assume that the age of fourteen represents the age of reason for children who can understand the danger of guns. That being the case, the push for legislative remedies to protect children from accidental gun injuries should hardly be an issue of major concern for the gun-control community. Nevertheless, laws which penalize gun owners for allowing minors to access workable but unsecured guns, known as child access protection laws (CAP) have been implemented in 29 states plus D.C.

Where both sides tend to find some common ground on the issue of gun safety is when it comes to training in the handling and use of guns. In fact, the whole notion of using a gun in a proper and safe way was first developed by a vociferously-determined gun promoter, Jeff Cooper, who published a book, *Principles of Personal Defense*, in 1989. The brief book begins with the following statement: "Some people prey upon other people. Whether we like it or not, this is one of the facts of life. It has always been so, and it is not going to change."

Note the book was published before Gary Kleck conducted his research which found that several million crimes each year were allegedly prevented because individuals had access to guns. Cooper's publication became not only the narrative which justified the shift from hunting to self-defense guns, but also became the pro-gun argument for getting trained with the safe and proper way of using a gun.

Cooper's approach to training was actually a self-training method which focused not so much on shooting techniques, but what he referred to as the 'readiness' required in order to know when to use a gun. Bering ready to respond to a physical threat with a gun was the basis for the training technique which Cooper developed at his own training facility which he started in 1976 behind a sand dune in Arizona which he then called Gunsite Academy, which is still going strong as a commercial shooting range following Cooper's death in 2006.

During his tenure at Gunsite, Cooper developed a narrative for readiness training which borrowed slightly from the Marine Corps and was based on the idea of thinking about situations in which protecting yourself with a gun might be necessary based on a color-code scheme which Cooper described as representing different levels of threat. The scheme was as follows:

White: Unaware and unprepared.
Yellow: Alert but no specific threat.

Orange: A specific threat has caught your attention.
Red: Ready to fight.

In all four categories, a handgun must be available and ready to use. This readiness also requires that if and when the gun might be pulled out and pointed at a threat (condition red) that certain safety rules are applied:

1. Gun must always be loaded.
2. Muzzle can only be pointed at a target you are willing to hit.
3. Keep finger off trigger until ready to shoot.
4. Identify target and what is behind it.

These four basic safety rules have been copied with slight variations in verbiage, by every gun trainer who runs classes on using guns for personal protection. In this respect, safety for the pro-gun community is basically viewed as a way to use a self-defense weapon properly, i.e., use it to defend yourself from an assault and defend yourself only against the individual who otherwise might be committing that assault.

The issue of identifying the threat which requires someone to use a gun safely and properly, however, was not treated at all in the interviews of armed crime-stoppers conducted by Kleck, nor is it discussed by Cooper or by other, latter-day, pro-gun trainers active today. Kleck's bigger problem, which creates doubt as to whether his findings can be taken at all seriously, can best be understood with reference to this story about an armed encounter which involved the manager of my retail gun store.

The store manager, Al, was a White male in his late 50's who was a truck driver and heavy equipment operator by trade, but also loved guns. He did his driving early in the day, then was in the shop most afternoons. His two sons were basically raised in the shop, except when they were in school or went home to eat dinner or go to sleep. Both boys ended up with full-time law enforcement careers.

One afternoon Al had to pick something up in a nearby town and was driving to his location when he stopped for a traffic light. There was one car in front of him, but when the light went from red to green, the car ahead of him didn't move. Instead, the driver, a big, Black man, opened the door, got out of the car, and started walking back towards Al.

What did Al do? He pulled a 9-millemeter Smith & Wesson pistol out and pointed it at the guy, who immediately retreated back to his car, jumped in, and drove off.

What we had here was a classic possible threatening situation which didn't become an attack because Al had a gun. This was exactly the kind of incident which Al would have reported to Gary Kleck as an example of defensive gun use (DGU).

Except it wasn't a DGU at all. Al drove several blocks beyond the intersection where the alleged DGU occurred, and all of a sudden, his car was surrounded and stopped by multiple police vehicles, guns drawn and pointed at him and over a loudspeaker someone was yelling, "Out of the car! Let us see your hands!"

The Black guy who Al had chased off by showing a gun had stopped for the traffic light and realized he was lost. He was coming back to ask Al for directions, but as soon as he saw the gun he drove off, got to the next corner, pulled over and called 9-1-1 on his cell phone to report a "man with a gun."

The situation wound up peacefully. In fact, one of the officers who had surrounded Al had purchased a gun in my shop. But if you look at the demographics of the individuals who allegedly might have criminally assaulted one of Kleck's respondents, or for that matter, the demographic profiles of the respondents themselves, there is no mention of race.

It is simply not realistic to discuss perceptions of violence and violent behavior without bringing the issue of race to bear in the discussion, particularly when Kleck's script that was used in every interview contained a reference to concerns about crime. Here is Kleck's own reference to using criminality as a basis for discussing the respondent's thoughts about engaging in a DGU: "Each interview began with a few general "throat-clearing" questions about problems facing the R's community and crime."

How do you conduct valid research into possible criminal confrontations in the United States and ignore the issue of race? You can't, you shouldn't, so you don't.

When he told the story for the fifth or sixth time later that afternoon, Al admitted that if the man had been White, it would never have occurred to him to pull out his gun.

The point is that when it comes to the issue of training with a gun, it's not enough to be able to yank a gun out of the holster, point it at a moving target and hit what you are intending to hit. Before any of that happens, the first thing you must do is learn how to decide whether you should be even considering using your gun.

Notice that in Cooper's four steps which he claims must be followed for using a gun in self-defense, there is no mention of how someone should determine whether a gun should be accessed at all. Cooper's dictum on situational awareness put my friend Al in the orange zone – a 'specific threat' had caught his attention. But the man coming towards him wasn't a threat at all.

The training endorsed or promoted by pro-gun organizations and advocates considers safety to be a function of how well someone uses a gun to defend themselves, and as long as someone with a gun follows Cooper's four-point dictum for responding to a threat when a 'condition red' occurs, any discussion about the issue of guns as being safe versus unsafe products doesn't take place.

This is the reason the pro-gun community went to Congress after the publication of the Kellerman-Rivara articles on guns as medical risks and persuaded Congressional budget-makers to delete funding for gun research from the budget of the CDC. Following from Cooper's approach to gun training, it was and is still assumed that gun safety was intrinsically tied to how a gun was used in situations which required armed, self-defense.

How did the gun-control community develop an approach to gun safety which differs from the narrative developed by Cooper and other gun trainers who followed in his wake? They ignore the issue of *using* a gun entirely and instead opt for a definition of safety which is based on how guns should be kept physically apart from anyone who would be at risk to use a gun in an unsafe way.

Who shouldn't someone be able to access a gun? First and most important are individuals who cannot use or own guns because they have legal or social background issues which prohibits access to guns as defined by GCA68: felons, mentally ill, addictions – all 11 disqualifying categories listed on Form 4473 which is used to execute a background check.

Additionally, individuals who might be disposed to use a gun in an unsafe manner because of their current physical or emotional status must also be enjoined from having access to guns. This category obviously includes children of a minor age, who simply aren't old or mature enough to understand the issue of risk represented by guns or by anything else. Individuals prohibited from accessing guns should also include anyone suffering from depression and hence a candidate for suicide, or an elderly individual who is no longer in their right mind.

The gun-control movement has promoted two strategies to deal with preventing people whose behavior or mental status might create a serious risk if such individuals have access to guns. To keep children away from guns, 27 states plus D.C. have enacted child access prevention (CAP) laws, which mandate the safe storage of guns in homes with kids. As for preventing adults whose behavior might create risk if they are allowed to access guns, 19 states plus D.C. have passed extreme risk protection order (ERPO) laws, which allow a judicial authorities to remove guns from the home of someone whose behavior has been adjudged as creating a risk for the improper or dangerous use of guns.

The gun-owning community has found itself unable to be as vociferously against CAP and ERPO laws as it has been, for example, totally and unalterably against laws that would require the registration of guns. This ambivalence is largely caused by not wanting to appear to be callously indifferent to safety issues involving kids, but also driven by the fact that ERPO statutes are often utilized by women who have been threatened or abused by men. Of the 15,000 – 20,000 gun homicides which occur each year, less than 15% of the victims are women, but virtually all of the fatal gun assaults against females occur within a domestic or intimate relationship with a gun-owning husband or friend.

It should be mentioned in this respect that the gun industry and its public advocates like the NRA and the NSSF have tried to use domestic violence against women as a springboard for promoting more female ownership of guns. For the most part, however, the strategy has been a dud. At some point, Smith & Wesson even tried to market several of its small, concealable revolvers with feminine-like pink finishes instead of the usual deep blue or black tones. The guns sat on dealer's shelves and eventually were recalled.

What makes the issue of gun safety so far removed from any degree of agreement between the two sides is that like everything else having to do with guns, the problem immediately arises as to whether training and proficiency in the use of firearms should be mandated as a condition for gun ownership or left to the individual gun owner himself.

As of January 1, 2020, there were six states which required some kind of safety training prior to applying for a license to own a gun: California, Hawaii, Maryland, Rhode Island, Massachusetts, Connecticut, and DC. But safety and proficiency are two different things. I have taught the required safety course in Massachusetts and a student can sit through the entire course and never actually touch a gun. The issuing authority in Massachusetts, which is the city or town police chief, can impose a live-fire requirement, but this happens only in Boston and several other towns.

You would think that even if owning a gun did not impose a training requirement on the owner, who being allowed to walk around with a concealed weapon (known as concealed carry – weapon or CCW) would require some degree of proving at least a minimal proficiency for behavior of that sort. In fact, only 18 states now mandate proof of proficiency before an individual can carry a concealed gun outside the home, with 11 states issuing CCW permits without requiring any live-fire, and 21 states having abolished any kind of CCW permit process at all.[18]

Even in the states which impose proficiency testing, for the most part the test consists of shooting a minimal number of rounds at a stationery target, with some tests allowing the applicant to shoot at multiple targets until the necessary proficiency score is achieved. This sort of test is an insufficient method for determining someone's proficiency with something as dangerous as a gun. Such a test does not in any way help determine whether the individual who wants to carry a gun for self-defense is capable determining whether a particular situation represents any kind of danger or threat at all.

Recall earlier in this chapter (pp. 21-22) the episode in which the manager of my gun store believed he was about to be assaulted by a Black man while sitting in car at an intersection waiting for the light to change, when the potential assailant was simply walking towards him to ask directions because he was unfamiliar with that part of town. If Al lived in one of the thirty states whose laws include either a statute or a court tradition that allows someone to justify using deadly force to stand in place, the innocent African-American man who wanted directions to know where to drive might now be dead.

This type of misunderstanding about criminal intent and the resultant fatal shooting of a thirteen-year old by an armed man who suffered no adverse legal consequences for exercising legal, armed self-defense, generated national headlines following an episode in St. Louis, which occurred in 2015. The event involved a man who came out on the back porch of his home and saw what he thought was another man charging him with the intention of committing bodily harm. The man on the porch pulled out a Colt pistol, fired one shot, and his alleged assailant fell dead.

The alleged assailant was a thirteen-year old boy, who along with a fifteen-year old friend, had been riding his bicycle through a back alley when he saw the man's car parked in the yard behind the house. The kid jumped off his bike, jumped over the fence into the man's yard, and then proceeded to break into the man's car in order to scoop up some loose change.

The car's owner heard a noise in the back of his home and went out on his porch to investigate what was going on. In order to make his getaway back to the alley, the thirteen-year old jumped out of the car and as he ran around the front of the car, the car's owner believed he was about to be attacked. The gun came up, the shot was fired, the thirteen-year-old fell dead.

How come the man on the porch with a gun believed he was being attacked by another adult? How come when he was brought to trial for murdering a young teenager the case was dismissed? The answer to that question is provided by the fact that the shooting occurred at 1 A.M., there were no lights in the rear of the house and the man who committed the murder thought he was about to be attacked by another full-grown male.

Under Missouri's 'stand your ground' law, the presence of an uninvited individual on somebody else's property is, in and of itself, the justification for using deadly force. Since the shooter was able to prove to the court that he was unable to determine anything about the teenager other than the kid was in the wrong place at the wrong time, he could not be charged or convicted of any violent offense.

The shooter was convicted of violating Missouri's gun law because he had committed a felony as a young man and therefore was not supposed to be in possession of a gun. It turned out, however, that the shooter was the manager of a popular, fast-food restaurant which employed a number of neighborhood adults and kids. He was convicted of a gun charge but given a suspended sentence so that he could continue to keep the restaurant open even after killing a teenage boy.

There is not one single state which mandates proficiency and/or safety training either for a license to own a gun or a license to walk around with a gun which imposes any kind of training or testing that might determine whether someone who wants to carry a self-defense gun has the slightest ability to make a decision about whether a particular situation represents a serious threat or is nothing more than a minor tussle between two individuals who are often friends or acquaintances before the violent event takes place.

If we know one thing about homicides, it is that this crime is the most unplanned, spontaneous, and least predictable of all major crimes, primarily because it usually involves two individuals who have been getting on each other's nerves for a prolonged period of time, and then at some point, to quote Lester Adelson, "a gun converts a spat into a slaying and a quarrel into a killing."[19]

The intimacy of homicide is not just found in the murder of domestic partners, with the fatal victimization of women as 15% of all homicide victims, but in fatal assaults where both perpetrator and victim are males. As Marvin Wolfgang pointed out following a study of 588 homicides that occurred in Philadelphia between 1948 and 1952, more than half the murder victims precipitated the fatal assault because of some behavior committed by them, and for both victim and non-victim precipitated homicides, more than 60%

involved some degree of interpersonal contact between perpetrator and victim before the murder occurred.[20]

The personal nature of homicide analyzed by Wolfgang for Philadelphia is typical of homicidal profiles throughout the United States. According to the FBI, of the 7,119 murders committed in 2019 for which law enforcement reported the relationship between offender and victim, 81% of the fatal assaults involved some connection between the parties prior to the murder taking place.[21]

Much of the precipitating behavior of homicide victims represents behavioral variations of situations in which individuals either continue to threaten another individual who happens to be armed, or in many cases it is the victim of a gun assault who has refused to back away or back down. One of the worst urban disturbances in recent years occurred for more than a week in August 2014 in Ferguson, MO when a White police officer shot and killed an unarmed, eighteen-year-old Black youngster named Michael Brown, after the latter refused to stop coming towards the patrol car in what appeared to be a threatening fashion and was then gunned down in the street.

This shooting was the subject of three, separate investigations, including a federal task force and in the end, the police officer was found innocent of any attempt to shoot and kill Michael Brown without cause. The shooting provoked widespread property damage in Ferguson, along with massive public demonstrations as well as the appearance of some rogue 'militia' members who claimed to be walking around with their assault rifles to 'keep the peace.'

Altogether, the situation in Ferguson was a mess and, if nothing else, symbolized the fear and distrust between police and residents of inner-city neighborhoods which is all too common throughout the United States. But what witnesses basically told two juries plus state and federal investigators, was that the victim not only disregarded the command to stand in place but made several threatening gestures and then came up to the police car and tried to land a punch.[22]

The United States is the only country which follows the Common Law system out of Great Britain and yet sanctions the stand your ground behavior which under Common Law is a privilege reserved only for the King. Is there a connection between this anomalous legalism and the equally anomalous presence of more than 300 million civilian-owned guns?

By the time the Bill of Rights was attached to the Constitution, there had already been several court cases in which a 'stand your ground' defense was successfully used as a plea of innocence to a charge of aggravated assault. Yet in the colonial era, guns were not considered to be used for self-defense.

Rather, they were kept at home as weapons to be brought out for the weekly or monthly drills of the local militia group.

It is too facile and easy to make a connection between the existence of a 'gun culture' on the one hand and the existence of a behavioral culture which now justifies the use of a gun to stand one' ground. We need to reserve our answer to this problem until we arrive at the end of this book.

Chapter 3

How Do We Regulate the Regulators?

The first two federal guns laws passed in 1934 and 1938 defined the types of guns that law-abiding Americans could purchase and own, and the basic procedures which had to be followed by individuals who wanted to sell Americans the guns they could buy and own. The problem with both laws, however, is that there were no enforcement procedures built into the statutes and no law-enforcement agency identified to be the enforcer of these laws.

This is not surprising, given the fact that government regulation of American life was still basically a feature of local or state governments, with the federal government being responsible for national defense, collecting excise taxes and little else. There was no national banking system at the beginning of FDR's first term, there was no social security, no comprehensive income tax system, no welfare state, no clean this or clean that. Even the vaunted exploits of the FBI operating as a national police force only started to become recognized after the Lindbergh Act was passed in 1932.

The regulatory environment for gun makers and gun owners was created by a law that was first introduced after the Kennedy assassination in 1963 and was passed and signed by Lyndon Johnson just prior to his departure from the White House in 1968. The law basically did two things: it codified the definition of legal gun ownership by defining certain behaviors which prevented an adult from possessing a gun, and it defined procedures to be followed by individuals who wanted to be in the business of buying and selling guns.

As to the former, the law required that anyone who purchased a gun had to attest to the fact that he/she had not been charged with a felony, was not an addicted user of alcohol or drugs, had not been dishonorably discharged from the military, was not a fugitive, and could supply proof of age and an address in the same state as where the dealer was located from whom the gun was bought.

As to the latter, the dealer had to manage and retain the documentation which showed the details of how and when every gun came into his possession, how and when every gun was transferred to a customer or another dealer, and the details about the individual to whom the gun was sold. The

1968 law thus ended the personal transfer of guns across state lines, which had been prohibited for handguns since the federal law passed in 1938 but was now extended to long guns as well.

The most important aspect of the 1968 law, however, was the decision to create not just a regulatory environment for gun sales and gun ownership, but also to grant regulatory authority to a federal agency, in this case the agency known as the Bureau of Alcohol, Tobacco, Firearms and Explosives (ATF) which was first created as a tax-collection agency in 1886 when most of the federal government's revenues came from excise taxes, the first income tax applied to all wage-earners being introduced in 1913.

The 1968 gun law directed the Treasury Department and the ATF to create the documents that would be utilized to regulate the commerce in guns and this brought about what is known as the Acquisition and Disposition form (A&D) which is used to maintain information on how guns move from dealer to dealer or dealer to customer, and the 4473 form, which contains the detailed information on the legal history and relevant personal details (address, age, birthplace, gender, etc.) of the individual who ends up owning the gun.

This documentation must be held either in the gun dealer's place of business or in his home. However, as opposed to business records (bank accounts, invoices, insurance forms) that are the property of the business, in the case of the gun documents the dealer is only the custodian. The documentation is owned by the ATF and their agents can enter a gun shop or the dealer's home without prior notice or a warrant in order to review these documents at any time.

The difference between paperwork owned by a business and the paperwork which is used to keep track of gun transfers in a business known as a gun shop is a distinction which is often either confused or simply ignored in the debate about guns. But the regulatory activity of the ATF is basically confined to studying the paperwork generated whenever a gun moves from owner to another, both individuals meeting federal, state, and local legal requirements for owning a gun. Here are the two forms:

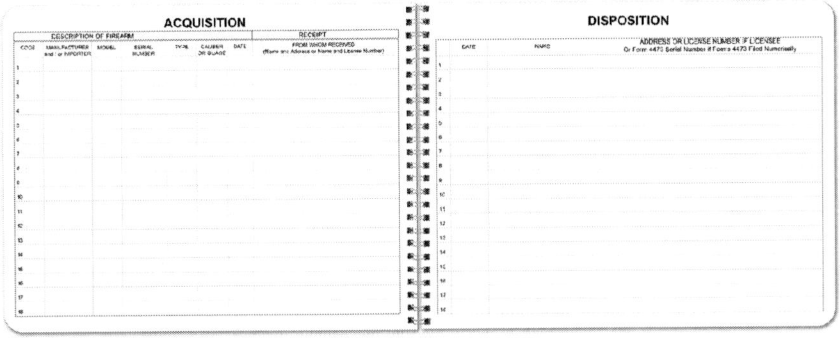

Figure 5. Acquisitions & Disposition book.

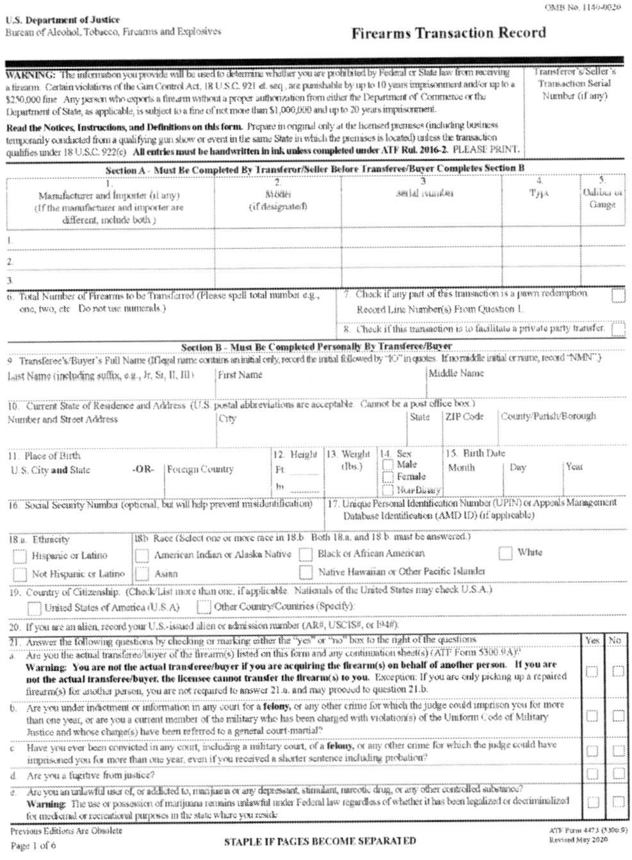

OMB No. 1140-0020

U.S. Department of Justice
Bureau of Alcohol, Tobacco, Firearms and Explosives

Firearms Transaction Record

WARNING: The information you provide will be used to determine whether you are prohibited by Federal or State law from receiving a firearm. Certain violations of the Gun Control Act, 18 U.S.C. 921 et. seq., are punishable by up to 10 years imprisonment and/or up to a $250,000 fine. Any person who exports a firearm without a proper authorization from either the Department of Commerce or the Department of State, as applicable, is subject to a fine of not more than $1,000,000 and up to 20 years imprisonment.

Read the Notices, Instructions, and Definitions on this form. Prepare in original only at the licensed premises (including business temporarily conducted from a qualifying gun show or event in the same State in which the premises is located) unless the transaction qualifies under 18 U.S.C. 922(c). **All entries must be handwritten in ink unless completed under ATF Rul. 2016-2.** PLEASE PRINT.

Transferor's/Seller's Transaction Serial Number (if any)

Section A - Must Be Completed By Transferor/Seller Before Transferee/Buyer Completes Section B

	1. Manufacturer and Importer (if any) (If the manufacturer and importer are different, include both.)	2. Model (if designated)	3. Serial number	4. Type	5. Caliber or Gauge
1.					
2.					
3.					

6. Total Number of Firearms to be Transferred (Please spell total number e.g., one, two, etc. Do not use numerals.)

7. Check if any part of this transaction is a pawn redemption ☐
Record Line Number(s) From Question 1.

8. Check if this transaction is to facilitate a private party transfer. ☐

Section B - Must Be Completed Personally By Transferee/Buyer

9. Transferee's/Buyer's Full Name (If legal name contains an initial only, record the initial followed by "IO" in quotes. If no middle initial or name, record "NMN".)
Last Name (including suffix, e.g., Jr, Sr, II, III) | First Name | Middle Name

10. Current State of Residence and Address (U.S. postal abbreviations are acceptable. Cannot be a post office box.)
Number and Street Address | City | State | ZIP Code | County/Parish/Borough

11. Place of Birth
U.S. City and State -OR- Foreign Country

12. Height Ft. ____ In. ____

13. Weight (lbs.)

14. Sex ☐ Male ☐ Female ☐ Non-Binary

15. Birth Date Month | Day | Year

16. Social Security Number (optional, but will help prevent misidentification)

17. Unique Personal Identification Number (UPIN) or Appeals Management Database Identification (AMD ID) (if applicable)

18.a. Ethnicity
☐ Hispanic or Latino
☐ Not Hispanic or Latino

18.b. Race (Select one or more race in 18.b. Both 18.a. and 18.b. must be answered.)
☐ American Indian or Alaska Native ☐ Black or African American ☐ White
☐ Asian ☐ Native Hawaiian or Other Pacific Islander

19. Country of Citizenship: (Check/List more than one, if applicable. Nationals of the United States may check U.S.A.)
☐ United States of America (U.S.A.) ☐ Other Country/Countries (Specify):

20. If you are an alien, record your U.S.-issued alien or admission number (AR#, USCIS#, or I94#):

21. Answer the following questions by checking or marking either the "yes" or "no" box to the right of the questions.	Yes	No
a. Are you the actual transferee/buyer of the firearm(s) listed on this form and any continuation sheet(s) (ATF Form 5300.9A)? **Warning: You are not the actual transferee/buyer if you are acquiring the firearm(s) on behalf of another person. If you are not the actual transferee/buyer, the licensee cannot transfer the firearm(s) to you.** Exception: If you are only picking up a repaired firearm(s) for another person, you are not required to answer 21.a. and may proceed to question 21.b.	☐	☐
b. Are you under indictment or information in any court for a **felony**, or any other crime for which the judge could imprison you for more than one year, or are you a current member of the military who has been charged with violation(s) of the Uniform Code of Military Justice and whose charge(s) have been referred to a general court-martial?	☐	☐
c. Have you ever been convicted in any court, including a military court, of a **felony**, or any other crime for which the judge could have imprisoned you for more than one year, even if you received a shorter sentence including probation?	☐	☐
d. Are you a fugitive from justice?	☐	☐
e. Are you an unlawful user of, or addicted to, marijuana or any depressant, stimulant, narcotic drug, or any other controlled substance? **Warning:** The use or possession of marijuana remains unlawful under Federal law regardless of whether it has been legalized or decriminalized for medicinal or recreational purposes in the state where you reside.	☐	☐

Previous Editions Are Obsolete
Page 1 of 6
STAPLE IF PAGES BECOME SEPARATED
ATF Form 4473 (5300.9)
Revised May 2020

Figure 6. 4473 Background check form.

An examination of these two forms, which define almost the entire regulatory activity of the ATF, is the point at which the whole story of how the ATF describes its regulatory mission and behavior begins to break down. Under the 1968 gun law and subsequent modifications, any mistake in either of these forms, no matter how insignificant, is defined as a violation of federal law, a felony punishable by five years in jail. So, for example, if a retail customer fills out a 4473 form and simply misses one of the nearly 40 fields that must be filled out, the dealer can be charged with a felony if he doesn't catch the mistake and make sure that every, single piece of information required on a 4473 form is listed correctly at the time of the sale. If the information in the A&D book covering a particular gun which is then sold to a customer does not exactly correspond with the information in the A&D book covering that gun, again the dealer can be charged with a federal crime.

In fact, except in a few very rare situations, what happens when the ATF inspector discovers a mistake in either a 4473 form or the A&D book, or discovers that a gun has entered and left the shop without both forms being filled out correctly, is that the dealer will be told to correct the form and if the requisite information cannot be found, the dealer will be required to contact the ATF office in Atlanta where the information about the missing weapon is then listed in what is known as the 'missing-stolen' list. In theory, any police department can contact this office if they are engaged in a criminal investigation which requires information about a particular gun, but rarely are such requests ever made.

The ATF spends a great deal of time promoting itself as an important cog in the fight against crime, particularly when it comes to the issue of tracking guns that may have been used in crimes. The process is known as 'tracing,' a procedure conducted by the ATF's National Tracing Center in West Virginia, which conducts more than 300,000 gun traces every year. All traces are initiated by a request from a law-enforcement agency which identifies both the weapon whose provenance needs to be learned, as well as the reason for the trace.

The ATF takes this information and contacts the manufacturer of the gun with its unique serial number and other identifying marks. The gun maker responds to the trace request with the name of the wholesale or retail dealer to whom the gun was shipped, along with the date of the first movement of that gun. The ATF then sends a second trace request to the wholesale or retail dealer who received the gun, and the recipient responds with information about the disposition of the gun after it was first received.

In theory, this means that every single gun which has been manufactured in the United States or imported into the United States since 1968 can be traced to the original retail purchaser of that particular gun. Unfortunately, used guns are not like used cars. They usually don't break down regardless of their age or how well they have been maintained. I owned a Colt1911 pistol which was manufactured in 1921 and it still shot perfectly in 2012, even when I used some Remington ammunition that was sold with the gun in 1921 as a promotion to increase Colt's post-war commercial sales.

The Colt factory in Hartford where the gun was produced has been empty since the 1970's, the Remington ammunition factory in Bridgeport has been a crumbling, red-brick shell since I don't know when and neither does anyone else. But the gun and the ammunition both work well.

The ATF claims that its tracing service would be more helpful to law enforcement if it could request information on more than just the initial sale. They state this explicitly on their website and this statement happens to be a lie. I do not know what other word I can use when an agency knows something to be true and yet consciously says something else which is not true.

There is absolutely nothing in the 1968 statute or subsequent revisions to GCA68 which prohibits the ATF from asking a dealer to submit any and all information on the transfer of a particular gun, no matter how many times that gun has come back into the dealer's inventory either as partial payment on another gun, or as a trade, or as simply because the gun owner needs a new set of tires for his truck or the washing machine needs to be replaced and a gun has to be sold.

One of the major demands of the gun-control community is to require that every transfer of a gun be validated through a background check conducted by a licensed dealer, a process which is now followed in ten states plus D.C. Therefore, if one individual sells or gives a gun to someone else in any state other than California, Colorado, Delaware, Maryland, Nevada, New York, Oregon, Pennsylvania, Rhode Island, Washington, and D.C., to all intents and purposes the ability to figure out how a gun went from the counter top to a crime scene ends at the initial point of sale.

But even in the states where private gun transfers are required to be performed in a licensed gun shop with a background check, the ATF wouldn't be able to furnish a police department with information about secondary or tertiary transfers because they only review the first time a gun leaves a dealer's inventory and is placed in private hands.

The failure of the ATF to look beyond the initial disposition of a gun not only makes it more difficult for police agencies to solve crimes involving the use of guns, but it also renders the value of another so-called crime-fighting tool of the ATF negligible at best. I am referring to what the ATF calls its Time to Crime (TTC) calculation, which is based on the number of years between when a gun leaves a gun shop for the first time and when that same gun is later picked up at the scene of a crime - or more precisely, the date when the relevant police agency sends the ATF a request to conduct a trace of that gun.

The ATF keeps records on this issue on a state-by-state basis, and currently the average TTC for the entire country is somewhere around nine years. Roughly ten percent of all traced guns wind up at a crime scene within one year after the initial sale, and when the ATF notices a surge in short-time TTC from a particular dealer, this individual is headed for a visit by an ATF inspection team.

But given the fact that the inventory of most gun shops consists of 30% - 40% used guns, the idea of creating a regulatory strategy around TTC measurements makes little, or no sense. Further, it should be noted that of the more than 300,000 – 400,000 traces conducted by the ATF each year, less than 20% involve guns that have been connected to serious crimes. Of the 393,212 traces conducted in 2020, the two largest categories for requests were 'found guns' and 'possession of weapon,' the latter meaning someone who did not possess the required license for ownership of a particular gun. Guns traced in cases of aggravated assault accounted for 4% of all trace requests.[23]

When the ATF shifts its emphasis from regulation to law enforcement, the results are spectacular – spectacularly bad. I am referring first to the 1993 siege of the Branch Davidian compound outside of Waco, which resulted in 86 deaths, of whom 4 were ATF agents and 82 were men, women and children who were members of the Branch Davidian sect.

The whole thing got started when a story started going around Waco that the Branch Davidians were manufacturing machine guns in their compound and were planning to use these guns to invade Waco and then touch off a worldwide, Armageddon-like assault. The local cops called the ATF who rented a house across the highway from the compound known as Mount Carmel and proceeded to watch the comings and goings over a period of months.[24]

At one point an ATF delegation went to the compound, knocked on the front door and were let in. They were given a tour of the site but did not view any equipment which appeared to be used for the manufacture of guns. The ATF also intercepted and studied the invoices of every, single item that was shipped to the compound via UPS and there was not a single invoice which contained items that could be used to manufacture or assemble machine guns.

In fact, the so-called eyewitness accounts about the plans for an invasion of Waco and the start of a worldwide crusade came from several former Branch Davidian members after they had either quit or been discharged from the sect. Numerous studies over the years have confirmed that such testimonies are suspect at best, and often fraudulent at worst. Nevertheless, the ATF not only believed these accounts, but put together an entire military-like plan to invade the compound and save Waco and the world from Branch Davidian wrath.

Just as bad as the massacre and fire which left 86 people dead was the fact that in the aftermath, not one, single individual who planned or executed this effort on the part of the ATF was terminated or even reprimanded. The post-siege investigation was a sham, the Democrats still controlled both chambers of Congress and everyone wanted to give a new Attorney General, Janet Reno, another chance.

If the Waco mess proved anything, it was only that the ATF had machine guns on their organizational brains. And this obsession with automatic weapons would provide the impetus for a second botched ATF effort, known as 'Fast and Furious,' which started up in 2006 and ended with the death of a U.S. border agent, Brian Terry, who was killed in 2010.[25]

Ostensibly, the ATF began this investigation because they had information about a gang in Nevada which was altering semi-automatic assault rifle into full-auto guns, then taking the weapons to Mexico for sale to the drug cartels. But behind this scenario was a second and even more pressing situation insofar as the ATF was trying to develop a crime-fighting strategy which would enable the agency to be granted permission to operate its very first federal wiretap, which previously had only been allowed for use by the FBI and the DEA. The lack of such a tool in the ATF investigative arsenal made the agency's senior management feel they were running a minor league operation compared to the other federal law enforcement groups. Hence, the 'Fast and Furious' scheme became the most important priority of all ATF enforcement efforts.

There was only one little problem, actually two problems. The first problem was the necessity to come up with enough semi-automatic assault rifles to create an interest on the part of the individuals who were thought to be willing to 'walk' the converted, full-automatic weapons back across the Rio Grande. The second problem was to locate and verify the warehouse and machine shop in Tucson where the assault rifles were being stored, then converted into full-auto machine guns and then loaded into vehicles for the journey to the South.

Over a four year period, some 2,000 guns were purchased by gun dealers in Phoenix and Tucson and then resold to buyers representing the Mexican cartels. How were the licensed dealers allowed to conduct illegal sales known as 'straw' sales with purchasers who had to pass background checks in which they declared that they were buying multiple guns for themselves? The ATF agents running the Fast and Furious program not only encouraged these licensed dealers to break federal laws which prohibited 'straw' sales, but in several instances made it clear to reluctant dealers that their federal gun licenses might be jeopardized if they did not go along with the program and bend or break the rules.

Not only did the ATF agents display a complete disregard for standard procedures which prohibited using law-abiding dealers to knowingly engage in illegal acts, but the ATF was never able to identify any physical locale where the alleged conversion of semi-auto to full-auto guns was taking place. The one location in Tucson which was ultimately considered to be where many of the conversions occurred, turned out to be nothing more than a standard auto repair garage which did not contain one single tool or piece of equipment that was needed to convert the guns – Mount Carmel all over again.

When this scandal erupted after Brian Terry was killed in a shootout with a Mexican gun runner who was using one of the illegally-purchased guns, the ATF now found itself the subject of a Congressional inquiry not led by some friendly Democrats who wanted to protect a Democratic administration from a political attack, but by a Republican-led investigation because in this second instance the Congress was now controlled by the GOP. But the decision by Iowa's senior Senator, Charles Grassley, to use his investigative authority to try and embarrass the Obama Administration over what the Attorney General and the President knew and didn't know about Fast and Furious relegated concerns about the ATF's performance to a much lower rank.

Ultimately, one field supervisor in the Tucson office retired (with pay) and another was transferred to a different detail. Not one individual in the D.C. headquarters suffered any blemish to his career. The only public official to be sanctioned in any way was the Attorney General, Eric Holder, who was the first AG in the history of the United States to be cited for contempt by Congress for allegedly misleading the investigation about the extent to which the White House engaged in knowing about the whole affair.

A year following the Fast and Furious Congressional investigation which went as far as the ATF went to figure out what had really gone on, a 160-page report on whether the ATF needed to be fundamentally changed was issued by the Center for American Progress.[26] The Center basically functions to provide research on policy issues being considered by the Democrats for legislative action. In this case the Obama Administration wanted to use the report to float a trial balloon about whether the ATF should be moved under the FBI.

The report was based on interviews with more than 50 current and former ATF staff, as well as staff from other federal agencies. It contains countless footnotes and substantial data about budget, staff, and activities, and it concludes by recommending that the ATF be moved into a subordinate position underneath the FBI. The report's basic argument is that the regulatory responsibilities of the ATF have suffered over the years as the agency has attempted to compete with the FBI and the DEA as an investigative and law-enforcement operation with the result that neither criminal investigations into gun crimes nor regulatory efforts over gun dealers are accomplished very well.

By the time the CAP report was issued, the Obama Administration had one foot out of the electoral door, so to speak, with Eric Holder already announcing that he was departing from the Justice Department to take a position with a D.C. law firm. So, ATF stayed put as an independent agency within the DOJ, and little, if anything was done to deal with the problems discussed by CAP.

The report is a typical CAP product – heavy on data, clearly written and referenced both to personal interviews as well as published sources. Unfortunately, as a study of the ATF's regulatory efforts and the controls it imposes over gun commerce, the report lacks any depth or perspective because there is not a single word in the entire document reflecting any contact between the CAP research team and the constituency – federally-licensed gun dealers - whose livelihoods and business activities are dependent on the regulatory efforts of the agency which is solely responsible for everything and anything having to do with the commerce in guns.

The report goes into great detail about the regulatory efforts of the ATF's industry operations division, the organizational structure within the agency which contains the staff that visits gun shops and conducts inspections to make sure that relevant paperwork is maintained in accordance with legal standards defined by GCA68 and subsequent gun laws. The report notes that cuts in the agency's budget has resulted in a decrease in the number of dealer inspections at the same time that the number of guns passing through retail outlets has doubled over the past ten years. This is viewed by CAP as a significant issue in the ability of the ATF to regulate gun commerce in a way that would help reduce crime and violence from guns, in particular the illegal movement of guns referred to as gun 'trafficking' from one state to another state.

The problem with this argument, and it is one of the reasons why the CAP report does not create any real basis for understanding either the value of the ATF's regulatory activities or provide a realistic basis for positive organizational change, is that most of what the ATF agents do when they come into a gun shop to conduct an examination of a dealer's paperwork has little, if anything to do either with the interstate movement or the trafficking of guns.

Most gun dealers build and maintain their gun inventory through a combination of trading or purchasing used guns from customers who then buy another gun, supplemented by purchases from several wholesalers who have usually been selling inventory to that particular dealer for years. The gun business at both the wholesale and the retail level is very personalized and is overwhelmingly based on the movement of products (guns, ammunition, holsters, accessories) between individuals who are personally acquainted with one another and who feel comfortable in business relationships with individuals with whom they have always conducted their business affairs.

My gun shop is located in a town with a population of 10,000, a population whose size has rarely changed over the years. It happens to be a town where probably three-quarters of the residents own guns, largely because the town has supplied workers to three gun factories which are all located within 25 miles of my shop. There are retail gun stores in the two towns that are adjacent to my town, and the gun owners in all three communities run back and forth between these three shops looking for the best deal whenever they buy a gun.

The big store chains like Wal Mart also sell guns, but their inventories tend to be restricted to rifles and shotguns because handguns are considered to be a risk, given the ease with which they can be stolen as well as the fact that handguns are usually the weapon of choice when it comes to the commission of an armed crime. What this adds up to is the fact that when the ATF engages in regulatory activity, just about their entire effort focuses on the transfer of guns between gun dealers and consumers, most of whom are known to the dealer and usually live within a short distance from the shop.

I once did a quick study of the geography of my gun shop's market by looking at the residential zip codes of some 500 individuals who had purchased guns from me over the previous year. Almost 90 percent of the guns which I sold to consumers went to people who lived within 30 miles of my shop. When I compared that finding to the addresses of buyers in a larger shop located at the other end of the state, this dealer was also selling most of his guns to customers who lived either in his town or in nearby towns.

From a Constitutional perspective, I'm not even sure the ATF should have any jurisdiction over the documentation in my shop and every gun shop that is created when a consumer purchases a gun – the Disposition side of the A&D book and the 4473. Since Federal law requires that anyone who buys a gun can only engage in a transaction with a gun dealer whose shop is located in the same state as the customer's residence, how come the federal government, as represented by the ATF, gets involved in these transactions at all? I thought the whole point of federalism was to restrict federal involvement in commerce to inter, not intra-state movement of goods, which happens to be a requirement for the private purchase of guns, and I do not see any text in GCA68, the law that created the ATF as a regulatory agency for guns, which makes mention of this fact.

This intrusion of the federal government into local gun transactions is precisely the reason why the gun 'rights' community has always taken a dim view of how the ATF operates, and notwithstanding the NRA's oft-stated claim about how 'law-abiding' gun owners always behave in a legally-proper and responsible way, the ATF is routinely criticized by the gun lobby and seen as just another attempt by the government to eviscerate 2nd-Amendment guarantees.

Things started heating up about the ATF in 1995 when Wayne LaPierre sent out a fundraising appeal in which he referred to ATF agents as 'jack-booted government thugs,' There had been an incident in which an ATF team had broken into a residence looking for some illegal guns except they had the wrong address, and the mistake made the local and then national news. What else was the NRA supposed to do? Ignore an event which was a perfect narrative to ask the membership for more cash?

The tone and content of Lapierre's letter was so nasty and extreme that it resulted in George H. W. Bush resigning from the NRA and making sure that his resignation was also a newsworthy event, including a copy of the letter published in The New York Times. But from the perspective of the gun-owning community and their supporting organizations like the NRA, Bush's response simply confirmed the idea that when it came to guns, anything having to do with federal gun regulations was bad, an outlook which defines the approach of gun owners up to the current day.

On the other hand, the gun-control community tends to regard federal efforts to regulate the gun industry from end to end, manufacturer to consumer, as not only a good thing, but if anything, an activity that needs more funding, more resources, and greater efforts on behalf the ATF. Some of this viewpoint is bolstered by studies which show that unscrupulous dealers are often the source for illegal guns, particularly dealers located adjacent to urban centers that suffer from high rates of violent crime.

There is also a constant argument made by gun-control advocates that the ATF is too lenient when it comes to sanctioning dealers who appear to be flouting the federal laws which describe the procedures that must be followed in every transfer of guns. Part of this concern is due to the ATF's admission that its enforcement agents can only inspect a small percentage of the federally-licensed dealers every year, a number which has never exceeded seven or eight percent. Yet this problem needs to be understood in the context in which it occurs, namely, that probably 70% or 80% of licensed dealer do not actually buy or sell guns except for anyone but themselves.

During the Obama Administration, there was a brief effort to try and produce regulations that would differentiate between federal licensees who were just buying and collecting their own guns versus licensees that were actually engaged in the business of selling guns. The initiative went nowhere so, at least in theory, every, single stipulation that governs the behavior of dealers in gun laws from 1938 and 1968 must be followed to the letter whether someone holding a federal firearms license sells hundreds of guns every year or sells none. Which also means that when the ATF discloses the number of annual inspections conducted each year, this number is compared to the global number of individuals holding a federal gun dealer license, a comparison which is absurd.

The recent gun law passed in 2022 contains a revision of the definition of dealer, clarifying I one sentence the idea that a gun dealer is someone who buys and sells guns with the expectation of deriving a profit from this activity. This revision was designed to differentiate between transactions which might affect the bottom line of a gun business, as opposed to transactions which represent an attempt by an individual to dispose of a private collection of guns. But since the ATF makes no distinction in terms of personally-owned inventory as opposed to inventory belonging to a business, regardless of whether guns are kept in a business location or kept at home, this so-called 'clarification' of the definition of a dealer makes little, if any difference at all.

My gun shop was inspected by an ATF team in 2014. They reviewed the paperwork – A&D book, 4473 forms – covering some 1,100 movements of guns in and out of my store. At the end of the entire process, which took several months, I couldn't produce paperwork which covered the disposition of three, whole guns. This doesn't mean that the guns had gone 'out the back door,' so to speak. It just meant that I had misplaced the relevant 4473 forms for two of the guns and for the third gun had forgotten to add the relevant notation to the Disposition side of my A&D book.

When the inspection was wrapping up and the paperwork for these three guns couldn't be found, I was told to call the ATF office in Atlanta and give the information to a lady who operated something called the 'missing and stolen' list. Were the three guns just missing or had they also been stolen? Neither I nor any member of the ATF team knew and nor did anyone care. What was important was to talk to the lady who ran the 'missing and stolen' list.

At some point following the inspection I received my official report from the ATF. I was informed that unless I came to a meeting in the office of the ATF counsel in Boston where all the problems identified in my recordkeeping would be reviewed, my license would be summarily withdrawn, and I could stop selling guns and maybe use my shop to sell something else. The report then listed more than 600 errors found in the documentation, each one of the errors representing a violation of federal law, punishable by five years in jail – for each mistake!

What were these felonies? There were several instances in which we abbreviated the county of residence of a customer on a 4473 form, there was also one 4473 form which the individual who filled it out didn't sign the form, and a couple of other felonious acts were found. But the biggest and most serious felony occurred more than 600 times, because we forgot to list the license number of the wholesaler from whom we purchased virtually all of our new guns, and usually forgot to list the wholesaler's address as well.

This particular wholesaler wasn't some guy driving around and dealing guns out of the trunk of his car. In fact, the wholesale company had been in business for 50 years, it was located some 20 miles from my shop, and it was inspected on a regular basis by the same ATF team which inspected me.

But as my inspection report pointed out, not only did every one of these omissions represent a felony under GCA68, but they were all considered to be 'willful' crimes because when we received our FFL some thirteen years before the inspection took place, we had been instructed on how to fill out the relevant forms. Under law, this meant that we were conscious of the fact that we were not only filling out the forms incorrectly but were doing so in order to avoid complying with federal gun law.

If I had decided not to go to Boston for a 'come to Jesus' meeting with the ATF, the agency would have stripped my license and I would have been forced to take the issue to federal court. The judge would have quickly overruled the ATF, my license would have been restored, and soon thereafter one or more of the gun-control organizations would have sent out an email to their donors complaining that, once again, a dealer who had been violating federal gun regulations had been let off the hook.

Going back to the CAP report on the ATF, what I found most interesting about the entire document was that it was based, in part, on more than 50 interviews with current and former ATF staff' along with staff from other federal agencies, but as I mentioned above, there was not one, single word in the entire text that represented any contact with the individuals whose business activities are regulated by the ATF.

How do you figure out what a regulatory agency is doing in the industry it regulates when you don't bother to talk about the agency's efforts with anyone from the community which is being regulated? And not only was there absolutely no attempt to look at the ATF's efforts from the perspective of gun dealers, but neither was this omission even noticed by any of the gun-control organizations which used this report to push for stricter government control over the gun business and more resources for the ATF.

Jack-booted government thugs versus overworked agency staff? The answer to both is no.

Chapter 4

Everyone Knows That Poverty and Violence Co-Exist

This chapter covers the true elephant in the living room when it comes to the issue of guns and gun violence, namely, the issue of poverty which in the United States is also the issue or race. Let's begin by looking at some data from the CDC.

From 2016 through 2020, there were 76,713 gun homicides in the United States, of which 45,688 victims were Black and 28,873 victims were White. The CDC stopped counting non-fatal gun assaults in 2016, but from earlier years we can assume that the proportion of Black to White non-fatal gun assaults was also about the same.

The national gun homicide rate from 2016 through 2020 is 4.70 per 100,000, compared to Western European countries like France, Germany, Spain, and Italy where gun homicide rates are somewhere between 0.8 and 1.9. The rate for White Americans is 2.39, per 100,000 White residents, for Black Americans it is 19.01. The latter rate is more or less equal to many of the Latin American countries, as well as some of the African republics, like Kenya and Cameroon.

Breaking the gun-homicide rate down by age cohorts, however, gives us a contrast between White and Black numbers that has to be seen to be believed. The age cohort which produces the highest rate of gun violence are the 20–24-year-olds. The White rate in that cohort is 5.12, twice the overall White rate. The Black rate for ages 20-24 is 54.26!

Other than El Salvador, which is the poorest country in Latin America except for Haiti, no other country has a gun-violence rate that is close to the rate for the 20–24-year-olds Black age cohort in the United States. For the next age cohort, 25–29-year-olds, the White rate drops to 4.56, the Black rate goes down to 48.34, again a rate which is outstandingly high for anywhere else in the world.

These gun-violence rates broken down in racial terms have to be set aside one other statistic, namely, the number of guns to which Whites and Blacks have access on a regular basis. We have some idea from the studies done by

Hemenway, Miller, Azrael, et al., which set the number for all guns owned by Americans at somewhere between 300 million and 400 million, give a few million either way.[27] Surveys on this question indicate that roughly fifty percent of White American households contain at least one gun, Black gun-owning homes appear to be slightly more than 30 percent. In other words, the roughly 50 million White households which contain guns produces an average of 11.5 gun deaths per 100,000 households from 2016 through 2020, whereas the roughly 5.6 million Black gun-owning households accounted for an average of 815 gun deaths per 100,000 households over that same period of time.

Why do we segment gun homicides by race? Because of all violent crimes, homicide happens to be the most *intra-racial*, as opposed to inter-racial crime. According to the National Criminal Victimization Survey, inter-racial violent crime of all types is less than 30 percent, with Black-White homicides at best representing less than 5 percent of all violent crimes. Moreover, according to the census, racial living patterns have become more, not less segregated over the past several decades, which means that gun violence is overwhelmingly an inner-city, racially-derived event.

As the demand for sporting and hunting guns began to stabilize and then declined in the 1970's and early 1980's, the gun industry began to push a marketing narrative which underlined the importance of guns as a protective strategy against crime. The first year that the entire gun industry manufactured more than 2 million pistols was 1993, which happened to be the year following the Los Angeles riot which broke out after four LAPD cops were found innocent in the videotaped beating of Rodney King.[28]

By pure coincidence, I happened to be visiting a gun shop in Baltimore the second day of that riot, which was April 30, 1992. The general mayhem in Los Angeles erupted the previous evening and at roughly 6:45 PM a video camera crew in a helicopter filmed and transmitted live video of four Black men pulling a White truck driver, Reginald Denny, from his truck, then beating and kicking him as he lay on the ground.

The Los Angeles riot was hardly the first time that a neighborhood was the scene of racial unrest in the United States. But it was certainly the first time that Americans could sit at home in front of their television sets and watch widespread urban violence while it was actually taking place. The gun shop that I visited in Baltimore the morning following the assault on Reginald Denny had a line of customers around the block. The owner, Mel Abrams, told me he had sold out his handgun inventory and couldn't get more guns because the wholesalers had also stripped their shelves bare.

Since the Los Angeles riot, the gun industry has relied on a fear of unrest, crime, and physical threats as the basic narrative for the sale of guns.[29] Here is the lead advertisement which the NRA ran in newspapers all over the United States in 1982, a campaign known as 'I'm the NRA."

Figure 7. I'm the NRA Advertisement.

And here are some of the ads that the NRA began running in the late 1980's, complete with stertorous voice-overs about 'dangerous streets' by Charlton Heston, who would become the NRA President in 1998 and would stand up at the 2000 NRA meeting holding a plastic replica of a musket in his hand and intone how his gun couldn't be taken away from his cold, dead hands.

Heston's speech underscored the decision by the NRA to promote itself and its membership not just as gun owners, but as *law-abiding* gun owners, obviously a contrast with all those gun-carrying criminals running around the streets. The comparison between 'good' people and 'bad' people in this respect also made it easy for the gun community to argue that gun violence could be reduced not by enacting new gun regulations, but by enforcing laws against violent crime.

How have gun-control advocates reacted to this campaign, which became even more extreme and overbearing during the 2016 'tough on crime'

Presidential campaign of Donald Trump? The basic response has been to push the concept of crime as a function of poverty, so if we want to reduce or eliminate crimes committed with guns, we have to end or at least mitigate the social disparities between the middle class and the poor.

Figure 8. NRA advertisements.

Unfortunately for the proponents of this argument, the fact that crime and gun violence is higher in poor neighborhoods doesn't necessarily mean that the individuals who engage in such behavior are necessarily the poorest of the poor class. A study conducted in the three emergency departments which serve the inner-city population in Flint, MI found that the socio-economic status (SES) of adolescents and young men who were injured in assaults and other violent events happened to be drawn primarily from an SES grouping that was *above* the SES population treated for non-violent injuries such as falls or vehicular accidents.[30]

Another problem which has yet to be acknowledged by the groups that are determined to eliminate criminality and gun violence by reducing poverty is that we have absolutely no idea exactly how many inner-city households contain guns. This is not a problem when it comes to estimating the number of guns owned by members of the American middle class for the simple reason that every one of those guns first entered a middle-class household when it was brought home by someone who passed a background check. And in states which require licenses either for gun ownership or concealed-carry, estimating the number of middle-class, gun-owning households is easier still.

The problem with connecting inner-city gun violence to the presence of personally-owned guns, however, is made more difficult for the simple reason that we have absolutely no idea how many guns are sitting in inner-city households for two reasons: (1). Licensing agencies often will not issue gun licenses to inner-city residents; (2). Many or the most individuals most prone to be involved with guns (i.e., males under the age of 30) have been convicted of criminal behavior which precludes them from owning legally-acquired guns.

Where do all the guns come from which end up being used in inner-city gun violence? We have absolutely no idea. There is no law in any jurisdiction within the United States that requires a gun owner to inform authorities of a loss of guns either because of theft or the simple disappearance of a gun. There is also not a single jurisdiction in the United States which requires gun owners to re-register their guns following the initial background check which, in and of itself, isn't a registration procedure anyway. Finally, although the police often send trace requests to the ATF, there is no jurisdiction which requires such reportage to take place, and the Presidential memorandum that was issued in 2013 by the Obama Administration mandating *federal* law enforcement agencies to trace all recovered guns has little impact on gun violence since federal agencies, as a rule, do not investigate community-based gun crimes.

The FBI estimates that somewhere around 200,000 guns are stolen every year, public health researchers have pushed that number to nearly 400,000. Note the word 'estimates.' The real, concrete number doesn't exist. There has also never been a study which shows exactly how guns move from the legal to the illegal market, even though the ATF publishes yearly data on the number of guns traced in each state which were initially sold to customers in some other state.

One of New York's senior House members, Carolyn Maloney, has been introducing a bill in every Congressional session since 2013, which creates a specific federal crime known as gun trafficking, a measure which ranks high on the list of favorite tun regulations for the gun-control crowd. The law was finally inserted as a section of the 2022 gun law and carries a sentence of up to fifteen years in jail for anyone who consciously sets up a scheme to get their hands on guns for resale to persons not allowed to own guns. This activity usually involves paying someone to engage in a 'straw' sale, then transporting the gun or guns to another state where it can be sold to someone who might then use the gun to commit a crime.

One of the reasons that gun-control advocates strongly support this law is because it reflects the degree to which gun laws are stricter in some states and less strict in others, hence, making it financially attractive to move guns from less-restrictive states to states which have more restrictions on gun ownership and therefore create a natural market for trafficked guns. This situation is often referred to in the media as the 'iron pipeline,' meaning that guns from Southern states move quickly and easily up Interstate 95 to more restrictive Northern states like New Jersey and New York.

The issue of when and how guns are trafficked across state lines made media headlines in 2006 when then-Mayor of New York City, Mike Bloomberg, sued 27 gun dealers in other states for aiding and abetting gun traffickers whose guns ended up being used in New York gun crimes. Bloomberg's suit was based on videotaped sales in shops where undercover agents purchased guns and made comments or otherwise behaved in ways that could have been considered proof that they were buying guns which would eventually wind up in someone else's hands.[31]

Although a majority of the dealers who were targets of Bloomberg's sting settled the lawsuits, and several dealers countersued, none of these lawsuits were ever argued in open court. But at some point, the internet carried a video of one of his teams engaging in a straw sale, and as a gun dealer I can tell you that the transaction looked harmless to me. The individual who was buying the gun kept turning to his alleged friend and asking his friend all kinds of questions about which gun he should buy. One could perhaps presume that the individual who was going to be the lawful purchaser of the gun appeared to be letting the other individual decide which gun should be bought.

This kind of behavior goes on in gun shops all the time because when someone who wants to own a gun but doesn't know very much about guns, the typical behavior is to bring an experienced gun-owning friend along to give the novice gun owner some advice. And if there's one thing that gun owners love to do more than anything else, it's to demonstrate their alleged gun expertise, particularly to people who don't know much about guns.

At this point in the narrative, we need to shift the discussion slightly and review an opinion issued in 2014 by the Supreme Court in *Abramski v. United States*, a case involving a former cop who was convicted of purchasing a gun for someone else, his conviction upheld 5-4 by the Court.[32]

Bruce Abramski was a former cop who lived in Virginia and at the request of his uncle, a resident of Pennsylvania, walked into a gun shop in Virginia, passed a background check and purchased a Glock. He then drove to

Pennsylvania, met his uncle at a gun dealer's store and gave the gun to the dealer who then transferred it to the uncle after running a background check.

So, both Abramski and his uncle passed background checks, but Abramski was guilty of lying on the 4473 form that he filled out in Virginia because in signing the form, he was attesting to the fact that he had bought the gun for himself. Why didn't Abramski walk into the gun shop in Virginia, pay for the Glock but have the dealer ship the gun to the gun shop in PA? Because the Virginia dealer was selling guns at discount to law enforcement agents, and Abramski used his police ID to get a cheaper price.

Did it occur to Abramski that he was lying when he signed the 4473 form which, by dint of his signature, made him the legal owner of that gun? Of course, he knew he was lying, he admitted the lie in court. But Abramski didn't believe he was trafficking the gun because he only gave it to his uncle after the latter passed a background check in another state.

When Abramski's attorney appealed his conviction to the Supreme Court, Associate Justice Scalia wrote a very interesting minority opinion stating that the statute governing the use of the 4473 form, GCA68, was extremely vague when it came to the issue of intent. But the majority opinion, written by Associate Justice Kagan, argued that even if GCA68 was less than perfect in defining whether an individual was consciously trying or not trying to evade the relevant regulation covering ownership of guns, to overturn Abramski's conviction would "completely undermine" the regulatory system devised to control the purchase and transfer of guns.

In fact, the vagueness of GCA68 when it comes to defining intent in how and why individuals buy guns, is matched by the degree to which there is absolutely no guidance published by the ATF on how a dealer should go about determining whether the individual standing across the counter is buying the gun for himself or buying it for someone else.

I can state that in my gun shop, and what I am about to say holds true for gun shops everywhere, is that over the years I have probably knowingly participated as a dealer in countless straw sales. For example, until Massachusetts revised and lessened its penalties for possession and use of marijuana (the state now has hundreds of public locations selling marijuana as a 'recreational' drug) there were many residents of my town and adjacent towns who couldn't purchase or own a gun because they had been caught smoking a doobie behind the school and pleaded guilty to an offense.

These were men who grew up, got married, had families, held jobs, never committed any real crime but also couldn't legally own a gun. The town where my shop is located is right in the midst of one of the best deer-hunting areas in New England – turkeys abound there as well. So, the wife comes in and buys the gun, while the husband stands next to her while she fills out the 4473 form.

Guess what? This woman has now committed a federal felony, and because I knew that she was buying the gun for the old man, I was aiding and abetting the commission of a crime, which is also a crime. If God forbid someone broke into her home, stole that gun, sold it to someone else who used it to commit a crime, the gun might be traced back to this lady and she could find herself facing the same kind of felony which Abramski faced when he stupidly tried to save his uncle a few bucks and bought him a discounted Glock.

The law under which gun dealers operate requires the dealer to insure that the individual who fills out the 4473 form is the person who is buying the gun for himself or herself. Is the dealer required to ask the customer whether he intends to keep the gun for himself? Is the dealer required to ask a customer why he is talking to someone else at his elbow about which gun he should buy? Is the dealer under any published requirement to ask a customer why he or she is buying a gun? Not only is the answer to all three questions 'no,' but most dealers would feel reluctant to ask such questions if only because it might be perceived by the customer as an invasion of privacy, assuming that the customer passes a background check.

The only requirement that a dealer must follow to verify the legality of sale beyond conducting the background check is to verify the customer's identity by examining and recording information from a government-issued, photo ID, said information (type of ID, relevant issuing number, likeness of photo) then inscribed by the dealer on the 4473 form.

I once got a call from the Chief of Police in my town who told me that he was sending over a bunch of guns that had been taken away from a town resident after the resident threatened his wife. The owner of the guns told the Chief that he was giving the gun to his brother who, in order to take possession of the weapons would have to pass a background check.

Now I happened to know both the owner of the guns as well as his brother and I can say without a chance of being contradicted that they were both no good. Period. No good. Nevertheless, the cops brought the guns over to my shop and the following day the brother shows up to go through the background check. Except the check didn't go through. It was put on a three-day delay.

Under GCA68 as amended by the Brady law in 1994, the guns can be transferred to the intended owner if three day delay expires but the FBI has not finalized the background check. This happens on occasion when the FBI gets an indication that an individual committed a crime in a state which for some reason doesn't respond to the FBI's request for additional information within three days. But the law also allows the dealer to hold off releasing the guns until and unless he receives a final response from the FBI.

Which is exactly what I did. I knew that the brother was not such an upstanding member of the community, and the fact that his background check was delayed only confirmed my belief. The guy came by the shop twice, got pissed off when I told him that I wasn't releasing anything until I received a final response from the FBI, and that was that.

Except it wasn't what happened at all. What happened was the next day I received a call from the local field office of the ATF and an agent told me to release the guns and note on the 4473 form that even without a final statement from the FBI, that the ATF had authorized the guns to leave my shop.

Why did I get a call from the ATF? Because this guy went down to their office, no doubt made a big fuss, and rather than listen to him yelling in the hallway the ATF agent figured that since the law allowed the dealer to release the guns after three days with or without approval from the FBI, so be it. Give the guy his guns.

The reason I have gone into detail about Abramski who didn't follow the law and the other guy who did, was to illustrate the idea that when it comes to keeping guns out of the hands of people who shouldn't be allowed to own guns, all the laws and all the statutes and all the regulations will have little, if any effect if there exists sufficient demand.

The sixteenth-century Valois monarchs in France were the first leaders of a national state to discover that if enough people wanted some product, a way would be found to satisfy their need. In the case of sixteenth-century France, the product was salt which flowed untaxed throughout the country no matter how many border guards and customs agents were employed to prevent this entirely illegal commerce from taking place.[33]

We have spent somewhere around one trillion, two hundred and fifty billion dollars fighting the 'war on drugs' since that war was first declared by Richard Nixon in 1971.[34] The death toll from drug poisonings is now over 100,000 per year, an increase from 50,000 in 2015. In 1972 the number was slightly less than 7,000 with a rate of 3.4 per 100,000. The 2020 rate was 28.3 per 100,000.

We need to pause here for a moment and state with certainty, that when we are talking about violence and criminality committed with the use of guns, we are not talking about the behavior of individuals who have law-abiding access to guns either as owners or users of guns. The Violence Policy Center has been tracking shootings committed by individuals who are licensed to carry concealed weapons, and in Florida, a state which has issued more than 2 million CCW licenses, less than 45 men and women were shot and killed between 2013 and 2020 by state residents with such permits.[35] Meanwhile, during the same eight-year period of time, the total number of gun homicides in Florida was 7,670.

What we do know about how and why individuals decide to use guns for crime and violence is that the interest in guns by individuals who end up involved in gun violence as perpetrators or victims begins when boys reach the ages of twelve or thirteen. Many of these adolescents will go into their later teen years and then transition into adulthood without being connected to gun violence either as individuals who use guns to injure others or are injured by others who possess guns. But for those young men who end up as a statistic in the yearly toll of gun violence, the interest in guns almost always first appears in the early teen years.

We also know that the young men who end up committing the most serious and violent criminality, a profile which first appears in the late teens and early 20's, have been what America's most foremost criminologist, Marvin Wolfgang, called 'serial delinquents' by their early teens. This delinquency is first observed in educational environments and most, if not nearly all of these adolescents drop out of school by ages fifteen or sixteen. A study of 99 Baltimore residents charged with homicide found that 98 had never finished high school.[36] Other studies have also found that the most violent youthful offenders (ages 12 – 17) constitute only 6 per 100,000, a rate which has dropped by two-thirds over the last two decades.

Why do a relatively small proportion of adolescent males become gun owners and users when all the adolescent male teens in any community are subjected to, and influenced by, the same social, cultural, and familial factors over the course of their brief lives? Not only don't we know the answer to that question, we also don't know how these various factors play out. Do video games make kids behave more violently when the game is not being played? Do hip-hop lyrics which often glorify guns and gun violence have a role in how kids behave? Are children more prone to carry and use guns if only one parent or no parents are in their homes?

Even if we knew the answers to those questions, there has yet to be any solid or even feasible strategies which could be implemented that would change the life paths taken by the young males who begin an infatuation with guns in their early teens and then end up either in jail, or dead, or crippled by serious injuries for the remainder of their lives.

The most frequent effort to reduce gun violence in inner-city communities is based on the idea that violence, like poverty, has social roots which need to be identified and mitigated on continuous and active terms. The program which sets a standard for this approach, *Cure Violence,* was founded in Chicago by an epidemiologist, Dr. Gary Slutkin, who started working to reduce gun violence in 2000 and has now taken his effort worldwide.

Slutkin's approach is based on the model that has been used for stopping and preventing infectious disease, which is to identify the source of the problem, isolate the carriers from everyone else and deal with the most highly-infected individuals on a continuous and comprehensive basis. This model with somewhat different variations, has been promoted by other organizations, in particular the work done by David Kennedy who joined with the Boston Police Department to develop a community-based anti-violence intervention campaign, *Operation Ceasefire,* in the 1990's.

The programs developed by Kennedy and Slutkin, along with other similar efforts rely primarily on either identifying violence-prone individuals or physical locations where violence often occurs, then sending individuals to intervene and shift the focus and energies of a potentially violent situation into more peaceful and productive ends. These initiatives have sometimes been successful, other times less so. The problem which all such programs face is that the moment the commitment to continuous intervention begins to lag, either because of funding shortages or difficulty in recruiting and training individuals to intervene in potentially violent affairs, the violence level rises again, or the violence activity shifts to a different spot.

The bigger problem with these programs is that they do not focus any energies or activities for ridding the highly-violent neighborhoods of their guns. In fact, if an intervener for *Cure Violence* is made aware that an individual who is confronted and prevented from committing violent behavior is armed, it is absolutely contrary to organizational policy to alert the police to the fact that a young adolescent is walking down the street with a gun.

As long as a community contains individuals who have access to guns for the purpose of using that weapon to kill or injure themselves or someone else, I simply do not understand how any strategy that will mitigate the impact of poverty and its attendant social ills will succeed in the long run. Like it or not, the young men walking around the poorest neighborhoods in our country do not share the middle-class aversion to violence because they view it as a basic means of protecting themselves from harm.

It is this view that creates the ongoing market for guns in neighborhoods where these guns then produce levels of violence and injury which are far beyond anything we find in other communities throughout the United States. Numerous surveys indicate that a majority of Americans believe that a home is made safer with the presence of a gun.[37] In communities where most of the gun violence occurs, the belief that a gun protects rather than hurts are also held not just about the home, but about the street.

If someone could explain to me how this paradigm can shift away from a reliance on guns which creates a seemingly unquenchable demand for such products, I await the response.

Chapter 5

Is Gun Violence a Threat to Public Health?

The CDC defines public health as "the science and art of preventing disease, prolonging life and promoting health through the organized efforts and informed choices of society, organizations, public and private, communities and individuals." Obviously, when someone is injured, the injury becomes a threat to their health, particularly when the injury is caused by a bullet shot out of the barrel of a gun.

Until 1997, the CDC gave out research monies to study gun injuries in the same way that they gave out money to study every other health threat. This support of gun-injury research ended in 1997 because two studies funded by the CDC which appeared in the *New England Journal of Medicine* in 1992-1993 found that access to guns in the home created an unacceptable rate of homicide and suicide and hence, a threat to community health. I discuss these articles in detail in Chapter 1 above.

In October 2021, the CDC announced that it once again considered gun violence to be a threat to public health, having awarded nearly $8 million in research grants the previous year. Yet when all is said and done, beyond providing some sought-after research monies which supports a group of faculty and graduate student researchers in various public health university programs, what is the net effect of declaring gun violence to be a public health problem?

The response to that question from public health proponents is that in order to reduce gun injuries, most of which are conscious efforts by armed individuals to kill someone else with a gun, we need to understand the 'root causes' of that violence in order to extirpate the problem at its core.

Unfortunately, what is left unsaid by the proponents of 'root cause' gun-violence research, is that it is very difficult to understand why a certain population commits a particular kind of behavior when the studies conducted on how and why that behavior occurs rarely focus on the individuals who behave in a way that creates this particular threat to public health. This is because the data utilized by just about every public health researcher attempting to understand gun violence happens to be data which is much more comprehensive in furnishing relevant information about the individuals who are the *victims* of gun violence, whereas the information at our disposal to understand how and why the perpetrators behave the way they do is both fragmentary and limited, leaving us with having to make conjectures rather than evidence-based conclusions about why gun violence actually occurs.

There are two sources of information utilized in just about every study of gun violence done under the rubric of public health. The first and most commonly-found data trove is the CDC's Web-based Injury Statistics Query and Reporting System (WISQUARS) which is a compilation of national estimates on fatal and non-fatal injuries updated once a year.

Fatal gun injuries are broken down by state and within each state the injuries are classified either as intentional or unintentional, and within the intentional category are divided between assaults (homicides) self-inflicted (suicide) and individuals shot by cops (legal intervention.) The homicide category does not differentiate between shootings that are considered to be attacks versus shootings that are considered to be self-defense.

The WISQUARS database used to contain estimates on non-fatal gun injuries, but this category was abruptly eliminated in 2016 because the estimates were often admitted being more than 30% higher or lower than the actual numbers, which made those numbers too unreliable to be used in serious research.

Like other data published by the government such as numbers on employment, income, population, commerce and trade, this county is too large to create comprehensive data based on actual numbers from every relevant source. Hence, every government agency which publishes data tries to develop a reporting and analysis method based on partial reporting from sources which more or less represent a reliable profile of every source which accumulates such data over time. For the gun data in WISQUARS, this means putting together a 'representative' group of hospitals based on size and location which together furnish annual information that can be trusted and compared year to year.

Using the WISQUARS data to make any informed investigation about gun violence should at least acknowledge four basic issues which make this data less than reliable when it comes to understanding why gun violence occurs at all. First, by failing to differentiate between gun injuries that are committed for 'offensive' versus 'defensive' reasons, the data obscures any ability to determine why a gun has been used to cause an injury, as opposed to an injury which just happens because it happened. Injuries which involve both a perpetrator and a victim are totally and completely different from injuries which are caused only by the behavior or circumstances surrounding the injured individual (e.g., falling off a bicycle or out of a tree) and should not be lumped together in the same database or compared in any way at all.

Second and more important, given the fact that all injuries caused by assaults are also crimes, one cannot assume that the appearance of a victim at a medical facility with an injury caused by a gun necessarily reflects the reality of how that injury actually occurred. Many injuries that are the result of an assault, even gun injuries, are not serious enough to be life-threatening at the time they happen. Which means that the injured person may or may not want to draw attention to his medical condition because, particularly if the injury was caused by a gun, the cops will also show up.

Third, the fact that WISQUARS data is based entirely and only on information about the victims and not the perpetrators render the whole point about using this source for understanding gun violence suspect at best, useless at worst. The whole point of public health gun research, as the researchers invariably state in their published work, is to inform public authorities who are responsible for creating and implementing laws and regulations that will better control this particular medical threat. The use of public health research by legislative and regulatory bodies is a fundamental cornerstone of the entire public health philosophy and approach, but how do you inform yourself properly in drafting a law or regulation to control the behavior of how individuals behave when the data you are using to inform yourself doesn't contain a single word about how the individuals whose behavior you want to control actually behave?

Finally, and most important, by no longer aggregating or reporting non-fatal gun assaults, using the data which only covers fatal assaults entirely and completely misrepresents gun violence in every respect. This is because the only difference between fatal and non-fatal gun assaults is that in the latter instance, the individual who commits the assault didn't shoot straight.[38] Nobody picks up a gun, points it at someone else and tries to deliver a non-fatal wound. Which means that everything else connected to a fatal gun injury – participants, location, motive, outcome – is exactly the same for non-fatal gun injuries. How can you therefore render a valid analysis for a particular type of behavior when you ignore at least 80% of the instances when that behavior occurs? You can't or at least you shouldn't.

The other data source utilized by public health gun researchers is the National Violent Death Reporting System (NVDRS) which is also operated and maintained by the CDC. This database, which has been collecting data since 2000, contains data from all 50 states as of 2018, whereas the data in WISQUARS goes back to 1998. Nevertheless, despite its brief history, the

NVDRS attempts to aggregate data both from agencies which deal with victims and perpetrators, both groups the subject of analysis outside of medical environments, in particular law enforcement agencies and coroners or medical examiners.[39]

The problem with this data is that although it is based on reporting from sources other than the hospitals that report to WISQUARS, it is also extremely incomplete for two reasons. First, in most jurisdictions law enforcement agencies are pleased if they can identify the perpetrators of homicides 50% of the time. Second, even with advances in toxicology and other chemical-biological specialties, the average coroner's office renders an accurate cause of death less than 70% of the time, and particularly in smaller communities there is often a reluctance to specify the occurrence of suicides.

Along with major insufficiencies of data, particularly data covering perpetrators as opposed to victims of gun violence, public health research is also frequently hampered by a misunderstanding of the laws and regulations which this research is designed to clarify and help determine its effectiveness and/or needed revisions over time. Here are several examples of how public health researchers utilize definitions of laws whose efficacy they attempt to analyze even when they do not understand the laws at all.

Example number one: In 2015, the gun-research group at the Bloomberg School of Public Health at Johns Hopkins University published an article on the effect of the existence of a permit-to-purchase law in Connecticut which had been passed and implemented in 1995. The law was passed to bring Connecticut into compliance with the Brady bill, except that Connecticut, like some other states, opted to conduct the initial background check done by the state police which would then be forwarded to the FBI.[40]

According to the researchers at Hopkins, the Connecticut law required that any purchase of a handgun was held back until the state licensing authority conducted a specific background check and then issued permission for the customer to receive the gun, a process that might take several days. The point of the law was to slow down the impulsive decision to use a gun to commit suicide, hence preventing many suicides from taking place. The article estimated that Connecticut's permit-to-purchase law would reduce suicides by at least 15% compared to similar states that did not require any kind of pre-purchase permit prior to buying a handgun.

This article was ballyhooed all over the place and became a standard reference for any and all legislative or advocacy groups which wanted to see PTP licensing in other states.

There was only one problem, however. The problem was that Connecticut doesn't have a PTP process. When a state resident turns 21 years of age, he or she applies to the state police for a license to purchase and own guns. The applicant takes a gun-safety course (which I have given to several thousand Connecticut residents), submits proof of course attendance, does the fingerprint and photo business and barring some kind of legal issue, receives the state gun license in a brief period of time.

Once the individual is in possession of a state-issued gun license, he can walk into any gun shop, buy every gun in the store, go through the standard background check, and walk out with all the guns. There is no waiting period, there is no advance permit, there is absolutely nothing which prevents a Connecticut resident from walking into a gun shop, walking out five minutes later with a Glock, sitting down in his car, and blowing his head off. He doesn't even have to go home.

When I asked a member of the Hopkins research team why they believed that Connecticut required a PTP prior to the purchase of a handgun, here was the response: "We got the information from Brady which publishes an annual review of which states have the safest gun laws."

Example number two: Currently, 29 states plus D.C. have laws which require that guns be kept out of the hands of children or other individuals whose access to a gun might create an injury or some other health threat. These laws, known as Child Access Prevention laws (CAP) are touted by gun-control groups and public health researchers as effective means of reducing gun injuries, both intentional and unintentional, along with illegal access to privately-owned guns, i.e., theft.

I happen to live in the state – Massachusetts – which has the strictest CAP law of all 50 states. This law requires that every privately-owned gun either be locked with an unbreakable device or locked away in a solid container or space which can only be accessed by individuals who have legal access to guns. If any gun is found in the home which does not meet one of those two secure conditions, the gun owner could be facing a felony charge.

Studies on the value of CAP laws to prevent or diminish gun injuries have been mixed, with some studies showing that gun owners are more diligent about safe storage after learning about the law, but whether the law has reduced the actual number of gun injuries does not yet appear to be true. On the other hand, what the researchers on this issue do not understand is that the courts have held that storing a gun in a physical location or with a device is not necessary if the weapon is under the direct control of its owner, i.e., if the gun owner can reach out and touch the gun.

Numerous surveys have been conducted by public health researchers which find that many children are living in homes where guns are not safely stored, but I have yet to view one survey which defines safe storage to include physical proximity of the gun to its owner or someone else who has legal access to guns.[41] In fact, when I asked members of the gun-research group at Harvard's School of Public Health whether they were aware that Massachusetts courts defined safe storage to include direct, physical control, they admitted that they did not know of the way in which the CAP law was defined in state courts.

Leaving aside the issue of whether public health scholars understand the laws and regulations on which they base much of their research, there is a much more fundamental problem involving how guns are studied by public health, actually two problems which need to be understood. To begin, the idea that gun violence can somehow be mitigated by making guns 'safe' either through redesign or more 'responsible' behavior shows a total lack of understanding about how guns are designed and how they are used.

The student who barricaded himself into a lecture hall at Virginia Tech in 2007 and shot 32 other students and faculty before shooting himself used a Glock pistol exactly the way the gun was designed to be used. Now the fact that this 23-year-old had what can only be described as a bizarre and unreal view of the world in which he lived (and died) says nothing at all about whether he used his gun properly or not.

Every technical and teaching gun manual begins by telling the gun owner that he or she should only use the weapon when the target is in clear sight and when he is pointing the gun only at the intended target and at nothing else. But the fact that Seung-Hui Cho, the Virginia Tech shooter, decided that the 32 people he shot and killed were legitimate targets for using his gun said absolutely nothing at all about whether the gun was being used in a proper way.

The companies that manufacture and market guns know exactly how their guns should be used and what constitutes a proper target for every kind of gun. Gun companies like Savage Arms design and manufacture guns that are marketed to be used for hunting and sport (target) shooting. Companies like Glock design and manufacture guns that are marketed to be used for armed defense. But what is a defensive use of a gun by one gun owner will be an offensive use of that same gun by the individual who is shot by someone carrying that gun. Who is to say which is which?

The second problem facing public health is that if the definition of their research is to create a pathway for medicine to align itself with public laws, then they have no choice but to define their research in terms of how it aligns and supports all laws, which includes laws which are used and justified to explain and promote violence caused by guns.

We turn to that issue now and spend a chapter talking about 2nd-Amendment ‘rights.’

Chapter 6

I Have a 'Right' to Own a Gun

The NRA describes itself as 'America's first civil-rights organization,' which would be true if the 2nd Amendment was, legally-speaking, a 'right.' But the 2nd Amendment is not a 'right,' even if it is found in the Bill of Rights. It is an amendment, which isn't the same thing.

Congress passed and ratified the 13th Amendment in 1865, which immediately transformed 4.5 million pieces of chattel property into human beings.[42] One year after the Amendment was added to the Constitution, the Congress passed the first 'civil rights' law to clarify the legal relationship of this new American population to all other Americans, which is why 'rights' are one thing and 'amendments' are something else – the former being utilized to define the latter.

Congress passed the first law to define the 2nd Amendment in 1934, a law which defined the word 'arms' as in 'the right to bear arms.' When the Supreme Court decided in 2008 that the meaning of the 2nd Amendment needed further clarification (*Heller vs. District of Columbia*) beyond how it had last been clarified in 1939, the 20,000-word majority opinion written by the Court's one self-described gun expert, Antonin Scalia, contained less than 300 words devoted to defining or discussing the meaning of 'arms.'

What Scalia argued was that the D.C. law which prohibited residents from keeping a handgun in their home for self-defense (or any other reason) violated the 2nd Amendment because America had a long tradition of allowing its citizens to buy and own handguns which could be kept in their homes in order to defend themselves if they were attacked. At the same time, Scalia also made a clear distinction between what he referred to as 'ordinary' weapons, which were protected by the 2nd Amendment, as opposed to unusual weapons or 'weapons of war' which were not deserving of 2nd-Amendment protections or 'rights.'

Since 1934, the Federal Government has enacted four more laws – 1938, 1968, 1994, 2022 – to further define the 2nd Amendment, but as in the case of the 1934 law, these statutes only pertain to gun 'rights' in terms of right versus wrong when it comes to how Americans can manufacture, sell, buy, own, and use guns. It should be added that for all the talk and complaints by gun-violence advocates about how the gun business needs additional regulations, I am not aware of any other consumer product whose use by consumers and sales by dealers have been covered by five very detailed federal laws.

Much of the 2008 decision which reversed previous definitions of Constitutional protection for personally-owned guns rests on the idea that America has a long tradition of keeping guns in the home, and by making a break with the previous legal framework for how to define private gun ownership within a Constitutional context, Scalia justified this new approach partially on what he referred to as America's history of a country where guns were considered necessary and useful implements for people who often lived at the edge of civilization and hence needed the security provided by access to guns.

Colt Firearms was founded in 1847, Smith & Wesson was founded in 1856. The last battle between U.S. troops and an organized Indian force was fought at Wounded Knee in 1890, the same year the U.S. Census claimed the frontier was closed. What this meant was that every square mile of habitable land in the Lower 48 had at least one permanent resident by that date. As late as the beginning of the 20th Century, thanks to the Homestead Act, Americans could still settle on what was basically free land.

By this point in time, the country now contained more than 160,000 miles of train track and more important, virtually all that track was of the same grade. Some of this construction was for small, local trains which carried residents from one town to another. But most of this mileage connected farming and ranching lands to urban centers for the movement of raw foods and energy sources, as well as to coastal cities where these goods were then shipped overseas. I live less than 20 miles from the Hoosac Tunnel, a 4.75-mile railroad tunnel under the Southern extension of Vermont's Green Mountain chain, which was opened in 1875 and to this day is used to haul freight from midwestern farming and mining enterprises to Boston where the goods can then be transferred for shipment up and down the East Coast as well as overseas.

Yet back in 1890, which is considered the start of America' second industrial revolution, the railroads connecting sources of natural and industrial goods were still running through what was largely unsettled, frontier land. Which is the reason Americans kept guns in their homes and just about every homestead beyond major cities contained at least one gun.

The near-universal existence of guns throughout every rural community in the United States is perhaps best represented by an event which occurred in the Missouri farming town of Skidmore in 1981. Here's Skidmore's main street today at the spot where this event, the shooting of Ken McElroy, took place:

Figure 9. Main Street of Skidmore, MO.

Skidmore is a farming community of some 250 residents, most of whom live on small, family-size farms around the town. The main street contains the town offices, including a one-room police station, a small credit union, a saloon (pictured above) a community social hall which is hardly ever used and a general hardware and farm-goods store which maybe opens for a few hours every day.

A railroad used to run through the town and stop at the freight elevator once a week. The railroad ended this service at some point although nobody remembers the exact date. Everything that everyone needs is down in St. Joseph, which is 40 miles to the South and is the county seat. The median household income is $30,000, which is half the median household income of the entire United States.

McElroy earned a living, so to speak, by driving around at night, stealing tools from various farms, then driving into Iowa, Kansas or Nebraska and selling the stolen goods in those other states. He had been arrested for theft many times but never convicted of any serious offense and the local cops tended to look the other way because he was always armed and had a quick and violent temper which got him into endless, physical fights.

In 1980, McElroy got into an argument with the owner of the town's general store, Bo Bowenkamp, and beat the 70-year old almost to death. Bowenkamp was the Mother Theresa of Skidmore. He gave goods to the farmers on credit when the harvest was late or small. He regularly served on every town committee and was always first in line to help.

Although nobody actually saw the assault take place, Bowenkamp's daughter saw McElroy enter the store and she discovered her father's bloody and unconscious body several minutes after McElroy left. He was arrested, charged, and convicted of this crime, but his sentence was suspended, which meant he was free to continue to terrorize the town. On July 10, 1981, a Saturday, McElroy, and his common-law wife showed up in town, parked their truck in front of the town saloon, went inside and started drinking beer.

While McElroy was inside thc tavern, a group of townspeople quickly met in the town's social hall to come up with some kind of community protection plan. A few minutes after the meeting ended and everyone drifted back down the street to the middle of town, McElroy and his wife came out of the saloon and got in their truck to go home. Several shots rang out, McElroy slumped dead over the steering wheel with a bullet through the head.

The shooting of McElroy was first investigated by the town police, then by the state police, and then by the FBI. When the feds showed up to try for the third time to identify the person or persons who had gunned down McElroy sitting in his truck in broad daylight and in view of at least 50 residents of the town, they produced no suspect at all. Everyone was interviewed multiple times, but nobody saw a thing.

Why didn't the FBI simply send the bullet which killed McElroy to their crime lab and then match the ballistics to a gun owned by someone in the town? They tried to follow this procedure to deal with what the media was calling an obvious case of 'frontier vigilante justice' but came up short partly because the slugs that were recovered at the scene were badly mangled, but more important, the type of rifle which loaded that particular type of bullet in that particular caliber (30-30) was a type of rifle found in just about every home in the town.

To this day, although the McElroy murder became the subject both of a book and a movie 'In Broad Daylight,' the crime will never be solved because all the witnesses and the shooter or shooters are dead. But the point of this episode is that guns like the gun used to kill Ken McElroy have been found in virtually every midwestern and western town because thanks to the Industrial Revolution such weapons were easily and cheaply made; and more important, the United States is the only country in the entire world which underwent an industrialization while most of the country's habitable land was still part of the frontier.

In fact, the technologies which were used by gun companies like Smith & Wesson, Winchester and Colt were for the most part both developed and first utilized by European gun makers, and what allowed gun designers to begin developing the kinds of self-loading guns such as the gun that was used to kill Ken McElroy was the invention first of smokeless powder by a German chemist, Christian Schönbein in 1846, followed by improvements in the chemistry of propellants by Alfred Nobel in 1891.

The major industrial innovation that came out of the Springfield Arsenal where the first assembly-line manufacturing took place in the United States was not anything having to do with how the guns were designed or produced. The innovation at the Springfield factory which quickly spread to manufacturing activities of all sorts, was the arsenal's development of a recordkeeping system which allowed management to keep track both of the orders and fulfillment with subcontractors for all the parts that were fitted on the guns, as well as a bookkeeping system which was used to determine the finished price of a gun so that the arsenal could bid on government contracts and still make a healthy return.

There were two reasons why Springfield was selected as the site of the first gun factory in the United States. First, George Washington owed a big favor to his friend and Massachusetts native Henry Knox, whose remarkable overland delivery of cannon from Fort Ticonderoga to Boston in 1776 broke the British siege and probably kept the colonies from losing the Revolutionary War.

The second reason for placing the arsenal at Springfield was that the topography of the Connecticut River Valley from its headwaters in northern New Hampshire down to the outskirts of Springfield had produced hundreds of fast-running streams whose water flows could be harnessed to create the energy required to drive tools used to cut both metal and wood. By the time Washington was able to convince Congress to spend monies on a government factory, there were dozens of small, manufacturing enterprises that could produce the parts required to be assembled into a working gun.

Even though the Industrial Revolution and the spread of cheap, mass-produced guns started to occur well over a century ago, we shouldn't underestimate how the legacy of guns being transferred from one generation to the next remains a fundamental reason for the existence of so many guns in American homes. A study by Pew Research published in 2017 found that nearly three-quarters of the respondents who grew up in rural areas had guns around them when they were young, even if they no longer live in rural zones today. This same study found that almost half the respondents in this nationally-representative survey who had at least one gun in their home was at least 50 years old.[43]

Generally speaking, gun ownership for most households with guns stretches back at least three generations, which means nearly one hundred years or not far removed from the early decades of the Industrial Revolution and the production of cheap, mass-produced guns. The fact that most of these guns were going out to families and households which were less than one generation removed from settling on the frontier, is a fundamental and unique aspect of America's gun experience which is never mentioned by either side.

The other unique aspect about American gun ownership is not so much the existence of a Constitutional amendment which gives individuals free license to own gun and keep them in their homes, but rather the reason we have promulgated five national gun laws to define those so-called gun 'rights.' It should be added, by the way, that the 2nd Amendment doesn't say anything about whether private gun ownership is predicated on being law-abiding or not – this caveat was attached to the debate over the 2nd Amendment by the pro-gun movement to make their argument about the necessity of guns qualified beyond reproach by the other side.

The United States is not the only advanced country to place private gun ownership under a comprehensive set of regulations which define the reasons why people can and cannot purchase and own guns. Most other OECD nation-states passed such laws either before or after World War II, in many respects these laws copied the first American gun law passed in 1934.

Yet the difference between legal American gun controls and the gun-control laws of every other advanced country can be found in the preamble of all our national gun laws, namely, the idea that the laws have been designed to aid law enforcement in their fight against violent crime. In every other country gun laws were passed as a response to threats to government authority coming from armed, mass movements and groups from the Right and the Left.

The United States is the only industrialized country whose government authority since the Industrial Revolution has never been seriously threatened by mass, political movements often mounted on the backs of massive and continuous acts of violence committed by activists who were armed. The Italian government that fell to Mussolini was overcome by organized, armed Fascist bands, the Weimar Republic lost authority for the same reason, the Second Republic in France was almost toppled by widespread manifestations of armed violence during general strikes, and the 1926 general strike in

England was a serious threat to the political hegemony of the Home Government as well.

The difference between the rationale for gun control within the United States – protection from crime – versus gun-control strategies implemented in other advanced, nation-states, is a much more compelling explanation both for which kinds of guns are subject to controls, as well as to concerns about infringing on 2nd-Amendment guarantees. Buying and owning a gun designed for hunting and sport is more or less subject to the same legal constraints in all OECD countries including the United States. Where the rules are different is when it comes to laws covering the purchase, transfer and use of guns that are designed for use as military or tactical weapons, i.e., guns designed to end human life, or what Scalia referred to in the 2008 decision as 'weapons of war." The fact that Scalia could make such a distinction in the *Heller* opinion shows how much the Court's so-called gun expert knew about guns.

But if I am going to take umbrage at how pro-gun advocates like Antonin Scalia didn't understand the subject of his concerns, the same could be said with even greater certainty about advocates from the gun-control side, whose incomplete argument about the 2nd Amendment – its meaning and use – is what brought the 2nd Amendment to the 2008 Supreme Court in the first place.

I am referring here first and foremost to an article which appeared in a 1989 number of the Yale Law Review, written by a noted Constitutional scholar, Sanford Levinson who argued that the 2nd Amendment couldn't and shouldn't be detached from the Bill of Rights, and if liberals were going to support other Constitutional guarantees like free speech and religious choice, then private gun ownership was deserving of the same support as well.[44]

Levinson also found himself in agreement with pro-gun advocates who claim thar an armed citizenry represents a fundamental bulwark against state tyranny and the use of state-sanctioned force to stifle political opposition or dissent. He states that the Chinese government would not have ordered the shooting of demonstrators in Tiananmen Square if those demonstrators had been armed with AK-47 assault rifles, which sounds suspiciously like the pro-un apologists who argue that Jews with guns could have prevented the Holocaust from taking place.

Levinson's belief that a bunch of guys walking around with AR-15's could represent anything that would in the slightest present a military threat to a modern, post-industrial state is tantamount to the bunch who showed up at the Capitol in D.C. on January 6th, 2021, to 'do battle' with the government that was in the process of transitioning its political leadership to Joe Biden and thus ending the governance of Donald Trump. The way Biden said it was like this: "If you want to take on the American government, you'd better show up with your F-15."

Levinson's article may have grossly overstated the efficacy of private gun ownership as a lever that could be used to give American gun owners a serious and necessary resource for thwarting the political preponderance of the national state, but his work was of sufficient importance in helping a movement of conservative lawyers bandied around the Federalist Society to use the 2nd Amendment as a means of promoting 'originalist' Constitutional ideas. The fact that the Supreme Court included a justice, Antonin Scalia, who was not only an active proponent of Constitutional originalism but was also considered to be knowledgeable and experienced when it came to guns, made the 2nd Amendment as a test of returning Constitutional legalities to their original meaning a perfect fit.

Scalia withdrew the 1939 Miller decision which granted 2nd-Amendment protection only to guns used for military service and replaced it with Constitutional guarantees for any gun traditionally found in the home, but he also left open the ability and authority of the government to decide whether any particular type of weapon should be considered a weapon for home use or not. The operative phrase was: "nothing in our opinion should be taken to cast doubt on longstanding prohibitions on the possession of firearms by felons and the mentally ill, or laws forbidding the carrying of firearms in sensitive places such as schools and government buildings, or laws imposing conditions and qualifications on the commercial sale of arms."[45]

Scalia then goes on to note that what he is trying to do is fashion an interpretation of the 2nd Amendment that will be a balance between a citizen's ability defend himself with a handgun in his home versus the authority of the government to regulate the types of handguns that can be kept in the home. He notes that the law which was the basis of this action enforced a complete ban of handguns which would violate 2nd-Amendment guarantees. But here is where both Scalia's view of the 2nd Amendment and the counter-argument by gun-control advocates departs from any degree of realistic knowledge about guns.

Take, for example, the current handguns manufactured by Smith & Wesson, the nation's second oldest, continually-operating gun maker in the United States (after Colt.) Currently, Smith & Wesson builds and sells 73 different models of handguns – 22 semi-automatic pistol models, 51 revolver models. All of these guns can easily be stored in a small, readily-accessible space within the home. All of them are fitted to load and fire ammunition of a caliber which is considered ample for personal, self-defense. In other words, if you want to keep a gun in your home that meets Scalia's definition for the kind of gun that meets his criteria for 2nd-Amendment protection, you can choose between more than 50 different types of Smith & Wesson guns.

What gives the United States a gun-violence rate that is 7 to 20 times higher than any other advanced nation-state is not the existence of the 2nd Amendment or the fact that Americans can keep a gun designed for personal, self-defense in their homes. It is the fact that some, but not all of the handguns manufactured by Smith & Wesson contain specific design features which are found on guns carried and used by military and tactical elements, features such as high-capacity magazines, bottom-loading ammunition loading ports, drop-button magazine release levers and frames cut for quick attachment of lights, lasers, and other tactical aiming devices.

These are the types of guns which currently account for perhaps as much as 75% of the fatal and non-fatal, intentional gun injuries suffered every day in the United States. In particular, guns that can load and fire in semi-automatic mode are favored precisely because they are replicated in all the shooting video games, are carried by military and tactical teams, and are featured in video and cinema because they can be fired almost endlessly as opposed to revolvers which have to go through a detailed and difficult reloading process after just five or six shots. Eliminating semi-automatic pistols from the civilian arsenal would not in any way violate Scalia's dictum for what constitutes 2nd-Amendment guarantees on guns.

Yet just as the pro-gun community reacts to any attempt to limit gun access based on gun design, so the gun-control community has similarly avoided any discussion about banning or limiting access to semi-automatic guns, for the simple reason that such discussions would be seen, it is believed, as contrary to 2nd-Amendment guarantees. Thanks to the influence of Levinson and other Constitutional liberals who are reluctant to challenge anything within the Bill of Rights because such a challenge, they believe would stifle or weaken their own defense of other Constitutional protections and guarantees, the entire debate on the 2nd Amendment has an Alice in Wonderland quality to it based on a thorough misunderstanding of how guns are designed and used.

The idea that an individual sitting in his home needs to respond to the threat of a home invasion or a physical assault by being able to fire a gun ten times before stopping to reload is absurd, and anyone making such an argument either knows nothing about the rudiments of armed, self-defense or about what constitutes a serious threat to life or limb inside the home, or both.

On June 23, 2022, the Supreme Court, in an opinion written by Associate Justice Clarence Thomas, expanded the definition of the 2nd Amendment to focus on the word 'bear' (as in 'to keep and bear arms') to mean that the Framers believed that access to a gun not only guaranteed Constitutional protection for home-bound handguns, but also protected guns carried outside the home. The ruling requires that the last 7 states which still grant discretionary authority to agencies which issue concealed-carry gun licenses now must issue such permissions solely on the basis of requests, rather than a stated need.

Here again, both sides in the gun debate argue from positions which have little, if any relevance to experience or facts. On the one hand, the pro-gun community which demands concealed-carry privileges because of the need for protection from crime, will not admit that violent, face-to-facc confrontations rarely occur in neighborhoods where residents legally own guns. The gun-control community on the other hand, decries concealed-carry as a threat to community safety when, in fact, individuals with legal CCW status rarely commit violent or personal crimes.

In other words, what we have in the debate over the 2nd Amendment is an argument where both sides promote views about what the Constitution says or doesn't say which have little, if any relevance to the issues which both sides believe need to be resolved.

We will now explore another area within the gun debate that is maintained and sustained by appeals to emotions rather than facts.

Chapter 7

Mass Shootings: What They Are and What They Ain't

The first mass shooting which made national headlines occurred on August 1st, 1966, at the campus of the University of Texas, when a 25-year old ex-Marine, Charles Whitman, killed his mother at their home, then drove to the campus, went up to the top of the tower with a bolt-action, scoped hunting rifle, and proceeded to kill 14 persons and wound 31 more. He was then shot and killed by a cop who went up to the top of the tower, snuck around to where Whitman was still using the campus for target practice, and ended the whole affair.

The man who committed this escapade evidently planned the event carefully over several months. But as Walter Matthau later told Bruce Dern, who played his partner in the movie 'The Laughing Policeman,' the shooter made one mistake. He figured out how to get up to the top of the tower, but he forgot to figure out a way to get down.

It turns out that most of the men who have shot their way onto the list of what Louis Klarevas calls the 'rampage shootings,' don't appear to be very concerned about whether they survive these events.[46] Perhaps the most noted survivor happens to be a man who committed one of the rare mass shootings which has taken place outside of the United States. I am referring here to Anders Breivik who in 2011 shot and killed 69 victims at Utoya, a weekend picnic spot in Norway, after killing 8 persons with a bomb he detonated in downtown Oslo. He now sits in jail for the rest of his life, having first been diagnosed as too mentally unstable to be tried for murder, then re-evaluated and found to be 'normal' which means that his incarceration must be reviewed and extended every five years.

Norway doesn't have life incarceration for homicide, nor does it impose consecutive sentences no matter how many victims are killed by a perpetrator at the same time. Had Breivik not been found mentally stable following a second evaluation by mental health experts, even after committing the greatest mass murder of all time in any advanced nation-state, by now he could be back at home and walking around the community as just another free man.

In the United States, we do not take such a benign view of multiple murders, or even attempted multiple fatal assaults. We are also in a small minority of advanced countries which still imposes an eye-for-an-eye punishment, i.e., capital punishment, for murders which are committed with intent to kill. But in a majority of instances when someone storms into a public space and dispatches twenty or more people with a gun, the shooter is on occasion killed by the police but more frequently takes his own life as well.

The two young men, Eric Harris, and Dylan Klebold, who murdered 12 students and one teacher at Columbine High School in 1999, ended their spree by killing themselves. The shooter at Virginia Tech, Seung-Hui Cho, who killed 32 people at Virginia Tech in 2007, also took his own life. Another suicide victim was Adam Lanza, who perpetrated the Sandy Hook mass shooting in 2012. Omar Mateen, who killed 49 people inside the Pulse Nightclub at Orlando in 2016 was shot by the cops.[47]

The fact that most of the men who commit these mass slaughters do not themselves survive beyond the event means that we only have scant evidence about the social and mental factors which combine in certain individuals to produce the moment when all rational thought and behavior gives way to this sort of devastating behavior. But the fact that an individual who is still alive after wiping out an entire community directly by mass murder plus indirectly by the residual psychological trauma experienced by everyone who isn't killed or wounded during the event, doesn't mean that any valid information about the shooter's motives or mental condition will ever be known and thus could be utilized predictively to identify other potential mass killers within our midst.

Almost all the perpetrators of the great rampage shootings used guns to which they had legal access, either because they purchased the guns themselves or were allowed to take a gun from another legal gun owner to use in their killing spree. The Sandy Hook shooter was legally entitled to take his mother's assault rifle to the school, even though he wasn't yet old enough to buy the gun himself. The graduate student who went into the movie theater in Aurora, Colorado, killed 12 and wounded 58 theater-goers who were watching a Batman movie was the legal owner of his AR-15, as was the young man who showed up at the Emanuel Methodist Episcopal Church in Charleston, South Carolina on June 17, 2015, and killed 9 members attending the weekly bible class with his legally-owned, 45-caliber Glock handgun.

Every one of these shooters not only used a legal gun, but both the Sandy Hook killer and the Aurora theater murderer had been treated extensively by mental health professionals before and during the time they were actually planning their rampages. In neither case did they disclose any relevant information to their therapists, nor were they even asked whether they had access to guns. The student who killed 31 fellow students and a faculty member at Virginia Tech, not only purchased his gun at a local gun shop, but he also came on campus that day with a chain that he used to barricade himself and his victims inside a classroom building, thus preventing the police from getting into the building while the killings were taking place. Meanwhile, the shooter had just been released from an overnight stay at a mental facility because he was considered to be no threat to himself or anyone else.

Before we get into more details about how and why these mass episodes of human carnage occur, we should insert some thoughts about how mass shooting are defined in the first place, because even on this issue, things just aren't that clear.

Mass shootings became a political issue when Trey Gowdy, a member of the GOP House caucus from South Carolina, submitted a bill in 2011, the *Investigative Assistance for Violent Crimes Act*, which was passed by both chambers and signed into law on January 14, 2013. Note the law was approved shortly after the rampage at Sandy Hook.

The purpose of this law was to provide financial assistance to local law enforcement agencies to investigate mass shootings, defined as an event which occurs in a public space and results in the death of three persons or more. To help clarify the term 'mass shooting,' since there is no specific criminal act which exists under such a rubric, the FBI began studying what the agency now refers to as 'active shooter' incidents, which means an ongoing situation in a public space which might require responses both by police and civilians that could alter the outcome of the event.

The point is to make a distinction between a homicide, which is almost always behavior that is dealt with after a dead body is found and the perpetrator is often far removed from the scene, as opposed to an active attempt by one individual to kill other individuals with the response by law enforcement or civilians occurring while the assault is still going on.

But in 2015 when the FBI published what it considered to be a detailed summary of all the 160 active shooting events which had occurred in the United States between 2000 and 2013, the list only contained events which resulted in a minimum of 4 persons losing their lives. And while the report stated that it had been developed as a needed tool to help law enforcement agencies investigate active shootings in response to the *Investigative Assistance for Violent Crimes* law, there was no acknowledgement that the primary criteria for defining a mass shooting as an active shooting event had been changed.[48]

Along with a definition of mass shootings as involving four or more victims, the FBI excluded the following types of events: (1). Conflicts arising from self-defense, (2). Gang violence, (3). Contained residential or domestic disputes, (4). Controlled barricade/hostage situations, (5). Crossfire or random fire as a consequence of some other criminal act, (6). Violent behavior tied to drugs.

What are we left with? Somebody has to walk into a public space, a restaurant, theater, school, and begin shooting at everyone he can see. But what if the shooter is high on drugs when he commits his assault? What if he wants to harm a specific individual or individuals but doesn't want the motive behind the shooting to be understood? What if he is a member of a gang but shoots both members and non-members of another gang or his victims happen to be members of a gang with whom the shooter has no conflict at the time the shooting occurs?

The moment you begin to qualify shootings as being mass shootings or not mass shootings based on a set of extremely vague and theoretical circumstances, you haven't really created the basis for developing pro-active tools that can be used to prevent or diminish the violence associated with mass attacks. This becomes an even more difficult problem when it then becomes the usual case that most mass shooters not only used guns which they legally owned or could access, but also planned the event for months or years without giving anyone else the slightest indication that something wrongfully weird in their lives and their mental disposition was going on.

Let's go back to the mass shooting which occurred in Norway in 2011.[49] At the time of this event, the shooter was 32 years old. He was a computer geek who worked and supported himself by doing IT consulting projects, lived with his mother and then alone and had no previous contact with authorities of any kind. He claimed to be a 'nationalist,' and was convinced that a worldwide war would soon break out between Christianity and Islam. His assault at Utoya was an attempt to ignite such a conflict while Christianity still had time to gather its forces together and win this war.

To give his world views some substance, Breivik had written and self-published what he referred to as a thousand-page Compendium, a rambling discourse on the histories of Christianity and Islam with the two religions in continuous conflict that can only end with one faith destroying the other. In Norway, as in other European states, the advance of Islam is aided and abetted by Communist and Socialist groups whose main affiliation is to an international, left-wing movement which also promotes anti-Christian and anti-White ideals.

Breivik worked in advertising and telemarketing both for various firms as well as twice starting such companies on his own. In 2006, according to business associates, he stopped working, moved back into his mother's home, and spent the next five years researching and writing the Compendium, getting involved with various far-right, racist groups online and planning his big attack. He also stopped seeing friends socially, isolated himself at home, and nobody including his mother had any idea what he was planning to do.

Breivik spent the next four years in front of his computer but was also ordering what he called 'survival equipment' from online suppliers and told his mother that he was preparing for a civil war. During this period, he lived on money he had evidently saved during the years he was employed, but despite his mother's suggestions that he go back to work, he never pursued any employment opportunities and rarely left home.

The psychiatrists who examined Breivik after the mass shooting declared him to be a 'paranoid schizophrenic' and a 'delusional psychotic' who could not be allowed to circulate in society because he was still a threat, if not to himself, at least to others. This assessment may have been valid from a psychoanalytic point of view, but these mental conditions in no way prevented Breivik from carefully planning and executing his mass attack.

On the morning of July 22, 2011, Breivik drove into downtown Oslo with a bomb in his car which he had built on his own with materials he purchased in stores and online. The bomb exploded after Breivik had left the scene, so it obviously had a timing device which Breivik had also made and attached to the bomb. The blast killed 8 people, injured 9 more seriously and more than another 200 persons sustained lesser injuries from the shockwave and destruction caused by a bomb that weighed more than one thousand pounds. The explosion also was Breivik's successful effort to divert the attention of law enforcement and safety personnel away from his next attack, which was on the island of Utoya which is some 23 miles from where he exploded his Oslo bomb.

Breivik took the ferry to Utoya, arriving at approximately 5:15 P.M. Almost immediately after parking his car, he began moving around the island with an assault rifle and ended up killing 69 people picnicking on the island and wounded 33 more. Within 7 minutes after the shooting began, police on the mainland received an emergency alert, but it took law enforcement another 65 minutes to arrive at the scene, at which point Breivik calmly surrendered his guns, allowing himself to be arrested without making a verbal or physical protest of any kind.

The reason Breivik chose Utoya as the site for his mass assault was partially because it was a small island which would make it harder for potential victims to flee, as well as for law enforcement and safety personnel to get to the scene. But there was another, more sinister reason Breivik went to Utoya, which was that the island was owned by Norway's Labor Federation, was used as a gathering spot for youth groups affiliated with the union movement, and Breivik considered the union and its members to be part of the worldwide Communist conspiracy which was trying to use Islamic immigration to destroy the White, Christian West.

Along with his delusional belief that his mass assault would precipitate a world conflict between the Christian West and the Muslim East, Breivik had another more self-aggrandizing motive for planning and executing this event. In fact, he had been trying, without success, to get his *Compendium* published by a trade press, and failing that effort, had begun his own personal online sales campaign. But the campaign yielded nothing to speak of, so Breivik saw his rampage and the consequent publicity as a strategy to promote sales. Both before and after his trial, Breivik actively worked on getting his *Compendium* noticed by the public eye.

The other mass shooting survivor, James Holmes, who killed and wounded 74 theatergoers at a midnight showing of a Batman movie in a Century 16 theater in Aurora, Colorado on July 20, 2012, didn't produce a self-promotion plan before or after the event. On the other hand, he was seeing a psychiatrist for months while he was buying guns at the same time. And like Breivik, when Holmes stopped shooting because his assault rifle jammed, he walked out of a back door of the theater and stood next to his car in the parking lot and was apprehended and arrested without incident or resistance.

Following this rampage, some pro-gun advocates made an argument that Holmes had gone to the particular theater because it was a 'gun-free' zone. In fact, there was not one, but two armed, out-of-uniform police providing security at the theater, but neither of them attempted to prevent Holmes from walking around discharging his guns. Their inactive reaction was because their police department did not allow off-duty officers to work as armed guards, and both cops knew that intervening with a gun against Holmes would result in disciplinary charges brought against them.

The big mass slaughters by men like Breivik, Holmes, Lanza, and others have certain commonalities, in particular the fact that in almost every event the shooter uses legally-purchased or legally-accessed guns. The shooters also tend to be loners who spend a great deal of time on the internet, often doing research on other mass shootings, or on political movements which attract their attention and whose programs are then cited as motivational factors in their decision to buy and then perpetrate mass gun assaults.

Yet even though the rampages which result in 30 or more deaths and injuries are what capture the attention of the public and the media, such events add very few numbers to the overall totals of fatal and non-fatal victims of gun violence, perhaps 1/10th of one percent of the annual toll. Much more frequent are the shootings which result in four or more deaths and injuries, a category of gun violence which has more than doubled between 2014 and 2021, the former year counting at least 269 incidents, the latter counting 611 events. Over this same eight-year period, the number of gun deaths other than suicides has also increased by nearly 60%, so it would be safe to assume that more mass shootings play a role in the overall increase in violent gun deaths.

Which brings us to consider not just the data on this type of behavior, but the reasons why such behavior not only exists but appears to be increasing all the time. To focus on this issue, we should look back to a shooting which occurred in Tulsa, Oklahoma on February 6, 2015, when two young men burst into the Gifted Hands barber shop, one of the pair spraying the shop with an AK-47 assault rifle, wounding three people inside the shop and killing the owner, a 41-year old man who was considered a fixture and person of repute in Tulsa's inner city Black community.

At some point during the fusillade, a young man sitting in a chair waiting to get his hair cut, pulled a gun out of his pocket, and fired one round at the man who was shooting the AK. The bullet from his pistol missed the shooter but went through the front window of the shop and pierced the radiator of the car driven by the owner of the assault rifle and his friend. They retreated from the shop, jumped into the car, and drove off, got about one block away when the radiator blew, the car stopped dead and the two occupants jumped out and ran off.

One of those two young men left his wallet behind in the car. The cops found the car a few minutes after the two miscreants had fled and with the forgotten wallet in hand, arrests were quickly made. Meanwhile, back at the barber shop, three wounded men were being taken off for treatment at a nearby ER, one dead man was on his way to the morgue.

Several days after reading about this event (which was later made into an episode on the reality-TV show *Cops*) I had a chat with one of the Tulsa police officers who investigated the shooting and made one of the arrests. He was a twelve-year veteran of the homicide and street crime unit and had investigated, by his reckoning, several thousand shootings over the course of his career.

What I didn't understand about the shooting inside the barber shop was that the two guys who showed up and started blasting away with their AK-47 were actually just looking to gun down one guy, who happened to be waiting to get his hair cut and also happened to be the person who yanked out a gun and returned fire which forced the two attackers with the assault rifle to retreat and flee from the scene.

"It was a small, narrow shop," I said to the cop, "so why blast all over the place and in the process kill an innocent bystander when you're just looking to shoot one guy?"

Ready? Here was the cop's response: "They always do that. They always keep shooting the gun until there's no more ammo left. It doesn't matter who they are trying to hit, the gun keeps going off again and again."

Whenever the TV news covers a shooting, you'll always notice that the investigators stick little, yellow, plastic pyramids down to mark where they find an empty shell casing in the street. They do this, I am told, because it makes it easier for them to reconstruct the shooting, particularly because in most street shootings, nobody saw nuttin,' if you know what I mean.

Marking the location of spent shell casings not only informs the cops about how the shooting occurred, but also alerts them to how many shooters participated in the event. I don't know whether the cops keep track of the number of spent shell casings they pick up at the scene of a shooting, but they do keep track of how many individuals are wounded and killed. We have those numbers for 2014 and 2021, and for 2014, there were 272 mass shootings of all types (public spaces, domestics, etc.) which resulted in 161 deaths and 1,025 non-fatal injuries, for a total of 1,186 victims of such events. For 2021, the overall mass shooting number jumped to 698, resulting in 705 fatal and 2,830 non-fatal injuries, for a total injury count of 3,535.

On average, a mass shooting in 2014 resulted in 4.36 victims who suffered both fatal and non-fatal wounds. An average mass shooting in 2021 created 5.06 victims, which means comparing 2014 to 2021, we have an increase in mass shootings of more than twice the number of events, but an increase in mortality of less than 20 percent. In other words, as the overall number of mass shootings goes up, the percentage of victims who are injured but not killed also goes up, a comparison which validates what I was told by the Tulsa police investigator about how the guns are just shot all over the place.

But even if the mortality of mass shootings is proportionately smaller as the raw count of mass shootings gets larger, these numbers hide a disquieting fact that needs to be brought out and considered not just in terms of understanding mass shootings but getting a clearer and more realistic understanding about the whole issue of gun violence in the United States.

Medical research about the effects of gun injuries is a fairly recent endeavor, particularly given the hiatus in CDC funding from 2007 until 2021. However, the preliminary work in this field suggests that individuals who are committed, treated, and released from a hospital after suffering a gun wound have a serious chance of being readmitted again for further treatment of either the previous injury or another medical issue which may or may not be related to the trauma suffered from a gun wound.

A study conducted of 183 patients admitted and then released at a Philadelphia hospital with non-fatal gun wounds found that the post-injury rate of alcohol and drug abuse doubled, nearly half the victims screened positive for PTSD and overall physical health of these patients was less than the average score for individuals in their specific age range.[50]

This study confirms what has been suspected by medical professionals who treat gun-injured patients, which is that the trauma from a gun wound is so severe, that even if the immediate injury is overcome and the injured patient leaves the hospital to try to resume a normal life, the possibility that further medical care will be needed cannot be dismissed. In several of these readmitted patients, radiologic examinations even found bullet fragments that had previously been overlooked.

The long-term risks to health of individuals who survive shootings underscores the degree to which the increased number of mass-shooting survivors must be placed in a proper context, namely, that surviving such an assault increases the possibility of greater medical needs in future years. Hence, the increase in mass shootings and the relative increase in survival rates should not be seen as a positive step forward in dealing with gun violence.

What the research on the medical outlook for mass shooting survivors also underscores are again the extremely limiting factor in u-violence research because most of our understanding about gun violence in all its forms is circumscribed by limitations imposed on studies because the research is overwhelmingly based on the *victims* of gun violence, as opposed to the *perpetrators* of this form of violence. This becomes a particular problem the moment we create a definition of mass shootings based on a completely arbitrary definition of 'mass' meaning four victims who are killed at the same time (the FBI's definition) or four victims both killed and wounded which has been the definition adopted both by researchers and gun-violence advocacy groups.

Why do both definitions fixate on 4 victims, either dead or dead and injured, as the defining number of individuals involved in what is then counted as a 'mass' shooting? There is no explanation anywhere in the literature which explains or justifies this numeric definition. In fact, it appears to have been first discussed at a meeting of specialists in 2005 who simply decided that four victims constituted a special type of shooting event which deserved its own category within the overall rubric of gun violence.

It might serve as a guide to understanding the motives and deigns of mass shooters if we had any evidence that these individuals planned their attacks to result in four victims, regardless of how many individuals were then gunned down. But there is no evidence of any kind which indicates that individuals who commit mass shootings have any particular number of victims in mind when planning their mass assaults. At the same time, if we define mass shootings only based on a specific victim count, can we really learn what's going on in the heads of the perpetrators when we lump together a shooting event where four individuals are wounded or killed along with another event in which twenty, thirty or fifty individuals are injured or lose their lives?

We do know one thing about mass shootings which is usually mentioned in a rather superficial and somewhat abstract way, which is that the weapons that figure in almost every mass shooting event are designed expressly for the purpose of being used to shoot humans and to deliver a maximum amount of ordnance in a very brief period of time. It is estimated, for example, that Adam Lanza discharged more than 90 rounds of military-grade ammunition at Sandy Hook Elementary School from his mother's AR-15 in three minutes of firing time or less. That works out to a shot fired every two seconds, which is pretty fast. Guns designed for hunting and sport shooting require careful and slow aiming and firing in order to be accurate out to hundreds of yards. In mass shootings, the average distance between the shooter and his victims is probably less than ten feet.

The proliferation of mass shootings, particularly the rampages where deaths and injuries mount up to 120 victims or more, has also spawned a cottage industry comprised of companies which either provide instruction for how to survive in an area where a mass shooting is taking place, or how to assist a wounded individual with proper, life-saving medical techniques, or both. There is also a federally-funded program at Texas State University which offers training to law enforcement agencies to intervene more effectively in events where the assault is still going on.

The Texas State University program, Advanced Law Enforcement Rapid Response Training (ALERRT) has been delivered to more than 140,000 first responders since it started operating in 2002, but for purposes of this book what is most valuable is an archive containing detailed data on 464 active attacks which have occurred since 2001.[51] The program defines an active attack as "an individual or individuals actively killing or attempting to kill multiple unrelated people in a public space," which obviously excludes domestic assaults, but does not qualify included events by the number or victims injured or killed.

What is particularly significant about the data covering these active killing events is the descriptions of what are referred to as 'resolution' of the attacks, meaning how the activity of the perpetrator ended, either because he committed suicide, was stopped by individuals on the scene, or was prevented from further activity by the arrival and response by police. In the 266 events which ended before law enforcement agents intervened, the attacker killed himself on 73 occasions (16%), left the scene in 120 instances (26%), and was stopped by on-site individuals 73 times, of which someone used a gun to either shoot or subdue the attacker 24 times (9%).

Every time there is a mass shooting at a school, the pro-gun movement promotes the idea that teachers should be armed and trained in the preventive use of guns. Obviously, there is no doubt that there have been more mass shooting events in school sites that might have been prevented or curtailed if a teacher or teachers in those schools had access to guns. On the other hand, of all the different reasons why a mass shooting in a school ended, interventions by armed school staff were less frequent than any other attack-ending method employed.

By failing to look at the one, overriding component that is present in every mass shooting, i.e., access to a gun specifically designed to be used in such events, an ambiguity is created in the research which flows over into the gun violence debate on both sides. This ambiguity and the problems it creates, will be discussed in the following chapter when we cover what Americans on both sides oi the gun issue know and don't know about guns.

Chapter 8

Is There an Anti-Gun Culture in America?

We know there is a gun culture in America. Its membership can be found every weekend browsing around the more than several thousand gun shows held every year, with perhaps 40 or 50 shows every weekend all over the United States. There are more gun shows where there are more guns, so Southern and Midwestern states may have as many as five or six different shows on the same dates, Northern states will have perhaps one or two. But on any given weekend, just about everyone living anywhere in the Lower 48 can drive to a gun show in a few hours or less.[52]

Over the years, gun shows have acquired a negative image which is largely undeserved. To begin, virtually every gun show is policed both by local law enforcement, agents from the investigative division of the ATF, and by representatives of the gun show promoter as well. The last thing a gun show needs to deal with is becoming known as a place where illegal guns change hands. If that kind of image gets around, at the very least the show will be cancelled, another venue must be found and the show promoter might find himself dealing with an investigation by the state police, the ATF, or the IRS.

Most gun shows rent tables and booth spaces to either legitimate, licensed gun dealers or to vendors selling clothing, books, hunting and shooting gear and all kinds of other products that can be found at many garage sales and flea markets which may have nothing to do with guns – cheap clothing, so-called homemade jewelry, art and deco products for the home, and all kinds of processed foods.

If you come to the show and rent space as a licensed dealer, you are required to follow the exact same rules for gun transfers that are followed in a bricks and mortar shop. A background check has to be conducted, a 4473 form has to be filled out and the form must also be designated as covering a transfer which took place at a show.

In states which still allow non-licensed gun transfers, individual collectors can display their guns and can transfer guns to others or buy guns from individuals as long as they follow whatever local rules on private sales might apply. Overwhelmingly, the same private collectors rent the same tables and booth spaces at every show, thc show managers know them well and can usually vouch for the honesty of such folks. For that matter, these private collectors also know most of the gun nuts who wander around the show because gun shows, like gun shops, tend to attract the same individuals all the time.

The reason that gun shows are considered threats to public safety and founts for the proliferation of illegal guns, is because the people who talk about these shows in the public domain – journalists, bloggers, public health researchers – are rarely, if ever connected to the gun culture at all. What they miss or simply do not understand is that just about everyone who pays ten dollars to walk up and down the aisles at a gun show is doing the same thing that people do who go to model train shows, computer shows, pet and animal shows, home decorating shows or wedding and honeymoon shows. All these shows are opportunities for vendors to sell products or services to a large audience and new customer base, or they are an opportunity for hobbyists in a particular hobby niche to meet, greet and talk to other hobbyists who enjoy the same things.

For reasons I am going to explain below, it is very difficult for someone who gets involved with a gun-control organization or activity to understand that the individuals, mostly fathers and sons but also some mothers and girlfriends, who walk around a gun show, have absolutely no idea that anything they are doing at that show is in any way connected to the 125,000 deaths and injuries which America suffer each year from guns. Walking up to the average visitor at a gun show and asking that individual how he feels about gun violence would probably provoke a response not unlike what someone would say who was walking around at a car show and was asked how he felt about the 40,000 thousand or so fatalities that we experience every year on our roads.

One of the major differences in cultural beliefs between gun advocates and gun-control advocates is how the two groups and the two cultures view the issue of responsible use of guns. To a typical gun owner, being 'responsible' means storing the guns safely at home and using them properly outside of the home, which basically means not giving a gun to an unattended child. To a typical gun-control advocate, on the other hand, being 'responsible' about guns basically means not owning a gun. The gun-control movement can dress up its narrative about 'respecting' the 2nd-Amendment all it wants, but there isn't a single gun-control advocate who would shed the slightest tear if he or she never saw or heard about guns again.

This dichotomy between the two populations, what I call Gun-nut Nation on the one hand and Gun-control Nation on the other, reflects most fundamentally profound demographic and personal differences between the two groups. In 2017, Pew published a detailed, demographic, and attitudinal study of gun owners (referenced p. 100 above) based on a 'representative survey' of 3,930 adults, of whom 1,269 said they were gun owners, which works out to the same percentage of gun owners in America which Pew claims to have learned from their research.

The study also cites the fact that 20% of gun owners are NRA members, which is an astounding number because it means that the NRA membership is somewhere around 18 million men and women, which is four times higher than what the NRA says are the number of members on their best day.

I don't buy the idea that Pew's research in this respect doesn't differentiate between actual NRA members as opposed to gun owners who consider themselves to be members of the organization because they agree with what the NRA says, even if they do not pay dues. As I am going to discuss in the Conclusion, it is simply impossible for a gun owner to claim NRA membership unless: a) he's lying, or b) the individual conducting the interview asked the question in a way which could elicit such a false response. But the fact that the NRA publicly discloses its membership number every month in the magazines it publishes should have given Pew at least some basis for determining whether this survey was or was not completely reality-based.

That being said, the other salient demographics about gun owners are well known and have appeared in countless sources over the years. Generally speaking, more residents of Southern and Midwestern states own guns than in other geographic zones, gun owners tend to be overwhelmingly male, married, above age 40, White, Protestant, living in smaller cities or towns, have a high school diploma or some technical college, earn $80,000 yearly, vote Republican and work in technical trades.

At the time this Pew survey appeared, I decided to conduct my own computer-based survey on the demographics and attitudes of gun-control advocates, research which has never been previously conducted or published by anyone. To that end I ran a survey using Survey Monkey and gathered 308 responses from gun-control advocates living in 44 states, the greatest number residing in California (37), Massachusetts (25), Nebraska (25), New York (25), Pennsylvania (17) and Texas (14). (https://mikethegunguy.social/wp-content/uploads/2022/06/GVP.pdf.)

Here are the answers to the demographic questions in my survey:

1. Gender:
   a. Male 45.45%

	b. Female	39.94%
	c. Other	14.61%
2. Age:		
	a. 21-29	14.29%
	b. 30-39	15.56%
	c. 40-49	19.81%
	d. 50-59%	19.48%
	e. 60+	29.87%
3. Education:		
	a. High School	7.19%
	b. Some college or technical	14.38%
	c. BA/BS	37.12%
	d. Graduate/Professional	52.31%
4. Household income:		
	a. $20K - $49K	15.58%
	b. $50K - $99.9K	50.13%
	c. $100K - $199K	25.32%
	d. $200K+	23.05%
	e. NA	15.91%
5. Living:		
	a. Urban	40.07%
	b. Suburban	46.69%
	c. Rural	13.24%
6. Religion:		
	a. Protestant	23.75%
	b. Catholic	10.34%
	c. Jewish	10.73%
	d. Muslim	6.9%
	e. Not religious	48.28%

The survey includes additional data on involvement in gun-control advocacy activities which we will discuss below. But at this point with what we have presented for basic life circumstances on gun owners from the Pew study and gun-control advocates from my research, it can be safely said that these two populations exist on different planets so to speak, if not in different universes.

The idea that representatives of these two populations could sit down and find common ground or even basic understanding about issues of common concern is simply not possible or even believable. Now let us take this line of research a little further and investigate not just the demographic differences between gun owners versus gun-control advocates, but also examine how these differences play out in terms of involvement in shooting versus gun-control activities, friendships, and events.

The major venues where gun-owning social activities take place are gun shows and shooting ranges, the latter often outdoor shooting clubs which also operate as membership organizations and provide weekend picnic and family-oriented events. There are somewhere around 11,000 commercial shooting ranges in the United States which together generate some $4 billion in annual revenues, but these numbers should not be seen as measurements which can be used to give us valid numbers of gun owners who pursue gun activities in any kind of regular or ongoing way.

Obviously, the most common form of gun socialization involves hunting, which although the sport is on the wane compared to other outdoor activities like trekking or kayaking, still engages at least 10 million gun owners, a number which we estimate based on the 14 million hunting licenses sold every year. Yet hunting does not tend to be a group or team activity and hunting clubs are also less extensive simply because open land in accessible areas has become less available over the last several decades.

Here again, the Pew survey has results which are somewhat difficult to sustain because one-third of respondents claimed to go hunting 'often' or 'sometimes,' which either means that they are not hunting every year or many gun owners are sneaking out to hunt without purchasing the hunting license which is required in every state.

One of the more persistent narratives surrounding culture, social activities and guns has been the alleged growth of interest in gun training related to self-defense. I say 'alleged' because while product interest in gun purchases has shifted towards self-defense handguns and away from hunting and target long guns, this emergence of what some gun enthusiasts refer to as 'Gun Culture 2.0,' has produced an increase in online and video training aids, but the purchase and use of such products does not engage gun owners in any degree of social interactions. In fact, this market is no more than a tangential element of the video shooting game industry which generates billions of dollars in revenues every year.

The gun industry is the only consumer industry other than the automobile industry which in certain states and jurisdictions requires some kind of training prior to getting involved in the industry by purchasing one of its products. But the training requirement varies from state to state, more often than not it doesn't even involve live shooting of a gun, and the industry imposes no qualifying requirements in order to become a trainer. Want to be a gun trainer? Call yourself a gun trainer.

Once an individual meets the legal requirements for gun ownership, this requirement is only confirmed again if or when the particular individual decides to buy another gun. If there is a single state which imposes any kind of automatic recission of personally-owned guns when a gun owner falls afoul of the legal criteria for owning a gun, such a state has been keeping said process extremely quiet over the years. Even the jurisdictions which now require that all gun transfers be recorded through the imposition of a background check, have no requirement that imposes a background check simply because someone has access to guns.

The Pew survey and other studies of gun-owning social activities reveal that using guns as a way to define one's social culture appears to embrace the most active gun owners in terms of how often they use their guns, but even in this respect the most frequent social interactions occur either at gun shows or at gun shops and hardly anywhere else. If a gun owner who lives in a Southern or Western state is asked which of his neighbors' own guns, he will probably point to most, if not all of the houses on his block. But all that tells you is that just about everyone in the South and West owns a gun.

In my survey of gun-control activists I also included several questions about social culture and the responses to those questions were as follows:

1. Do you own a gun?
   Yes 48.53%
   No 51.47%
2. Do you have friends who own guns?
   Yes 86.23%
   No 13.77
3. Have you ever attended a gun-control event?
   Multiple times 36.93%
   Several times 10.46%
   Once 6.86%
   Never 45.75%
4. Are you a member or supporter of a gun-control group?
   Yes 52.72%
   No 45.29%
5. How long have you been a member or supporter of a gun-control group?
   10 years or longer 15.79%

5-9 years	14.14%
0-4 years	28.95%
Never	41.12%

Taken together, the answers about socio-cultural attitudes and activities by both gun owners and gun-control advocates reveal that guns play a role in determining social and cultural attitudes and activities for some, but certainly not all the members of both groups. Beyond the issue of gun ownership, basic views about society and politics within the two populations are as much a function of education, income, work experience and geographic location as they reflect anything to do with guns.

Not only are guns not a decisive factor for determining the social and cultural activities and beliefs of the two groups, but other surveys we conducted showed a surprising lack of knowledge by both many gun owners and gun-control advocates about the legal and product-related issues connected to guns. On the one hand, a survey in which we asked 99 self-described gun-control activists whether they could define the difference between semi-automatic and full-automatic guns, whether they knew which age cohorts suffered the highest rates of gun injuries, whether they could define the relative medical cost of treating gun injuries as opposed to treating other types of injuries and whether they knew how many individuals were victims of gun injurie each year revealed that more than 75% of the respondents knew the correct answers to all or most of these queries.

On the other hand, we conducted a survey in which we asked gun-control advocates to respond to 12 questions which covered basic gun laws that have figured in most of the current political debates on increasing or extending gun regulations, and the average gun-control activist or advocate answered these questions correctly no more than 50% of the time. Only one out of five respondents answered the question correctly which asked them to explain the 2008 Heller decision, and less than one out of five respondents knew that the individual who underwent a background check prior to buying a gun had to be the same individual who paid for the gun.

When we conducted a survey answered by 285 respondents who described themselves as being supporters of gun 'rights,' this group overwhelmingly answered questions correctly which asked them specific questions about the design of guns, such as the difference between a single-action and double-action revolver or the difference between a semi-automatic and full-automatic gun. On the other hand, when this group was asked questions about injuries suffered from guns, such as the number of gun suicides suffered each year or the number of individuals accidentally killed or injured annually with guns, for both questions the correct answers were given by only one-third of the individuals who answered the survey.

Finally, we also conducted a survey in which we asked more than 1,500 respondents to answer questions about which gun laws or gun regulations should or should not be imposed on the public. We did not ask respondents to identify themselves as gun owners or non-gun owners because we wanted this survey to be a guide to how the 'average' American felt about gun control whether they were gun owners or not. Variations of this type of survey have been conducted by other researchers, but invariably those efforts ask respondents to identify themselves in terms of gun ownership.

I happen to think that such surveys need to be evaluated not so much in terms of how the two populations (gun owners versus non-gun owners) think about gun control, but whether the responses from both groups say more about their need to justify their stance relative to whether or not they own guns, rather than how they actually feel about specific laws which control the ownership and use of guns. Because this was a very important survey answered by a large respondent pool, it can also be downloaded here: https://mikethegunguy.social/wp-content/uploads/2022/06/gun-laws.pdf.

Taking the responses to the surveys mentioned above, what would happen if a representative group of gun owners or pro-gun activists sat down with a representative group of gun-control activists to hold a serious and substantive discussion about legal strategies to reduce gun violence? Notwithstanding the extreme disparities between the two groups in terms of education, income, location, gender, and other socio-cultural factors, they would find a certain degree of common beliefs.

More than seven out of ten respondents supported the idea of comprehensive background checks, more than six out of ten were in favor of an assault-weapon ban, a response that would probably be stronger today than when I conducted this survey in 2017. Six out of ten respondents also favored a ban on gun magazines which held more than ten rounds. Six out of ten respondents supported safe-storage laws, and 80% of respondents favored a required proficiency test before someone could own a gun.

Since the survey managers recruited respondents who were divided in half in terms of whether they were gun owners, clearly some gun owners supported gun regulations that are always listed as priorities by gun-control organizations and groups. But this survey also contains three questions which are always mentioned by the gun 'rights' community as being of importance to them. Here are those questions and how every respondent answered:

1. Are you in favor of eliminating gun-free zones so that people can protect themselves?
   Yes 52.83%
   No 35.44%
   Not sure 10.44%.
2. Do you believe that if someone has a concealed-carry license from one state he/she should be able to travel to any state with a concealed gun?
   Yes 58.63%
   No 41.37%.
3. Should gun safety be taught in K-12 schools?
   Yes 66.28%
   No 33.72%.

What this survey clearly indicates is that even though a majority of Americans do not own guns, a majority of Americans support legal initiatives which are not only anathema to gun-control organizations but are opposed by these groups because it is believed that all three practices would, if anything, tend to increase gun risk and therefore increase the rate and incidence of gun violence.

Furthermore, the answers to these surveys demonstrate that while there does appear to be some degree of shared beliefs about guns by people who own guns, the community which is active in gun control organizations has a very limited degree of contact within this population as a whole, and has less awareness of the politics, laws and outlook which impinge on gun owners than the degree to which gun owners understand the views and culture of the other side.

How do we go about redressing this imbalance? What strategies should be adopted by the gun-control movement to give itself the same degree of consciousness and cohesion which exists within the community that defines itself as being pro-gun?

The answers to those questions form the conclusion of this book.

Conclusion: What Needs to Be Done?

It is now almost a decade since Sandy Hook and the birth of a widespread, active, grass-roots gun-control movement. Over those ten years, at least 350,000 Americans have lost their lives through intentional acts of gun violence. With the exception of suicide using methods other than guns, no other intentional injury has been responsible for even 1/20th the number of deaths that have been caused by the use of guns.

Not only is gun violence the leading cause of intentional fatal injury deaths, but the gross numbers of victims and the rate of gun violence has increased every year since 2013, with the as-yet unpublished data for 2021 and 2022 no doubt showing even greater increased violence due to Covid-19 and perhaps other causes as well.

We have discussed in detail above (pp. 56 *et. seq.)* the limitations on research about gun violence, and while the 2021 resumption of research funding may yield some additional information which could allow for the refinement of certain explanatory nuances about the general issue, the fact that access to the perpetrators of this type of behavior is blocked whether because they are dead, in the case of suicide, or are unable to be studied because they are incarcerated, in the case of homicide, means that looking for a comprehensive approach to this problem by creating an evidence-based informational fount does not appear to be yielding any salutary results.

A further problem which has come to the forefront over the last decade is the degree to which laws and regulations imposed in jurisdictions where such activity does not run afoul of institutional or organizational resistance has not shown itself to make much of a difference when we compare the intent of new laws to the results after these new statutes are put into effect.

For example, five states passed much broader gun-control regulations after Sandy Hook – New York, Connecticut, New Jersey, Maryland, and Colorado – all five new regulatory regimes using comprehensive background checks as the basis for their expansion of gun laws. Three of these states, Connecticut, Maryland, and Colorado, saw substantial increase in gun violence rates between 2014 and 2018, in other words before the Pandemic appeared. Both New Jersey and New York experienced declines in gun violence rates, but the diminution in both states was very slight. It goes without saying that none of these states with their new, expanded regulatory environments escaped the extraordinary increase in gun-violence rates during the Pandemic years.

At the time, this text is being written (June 2022) the Supreme Court has just issued a much-awaited ruling on whether New York State's restrictive licensing of concealed-carry (CCW) violates the 2nd Amendment as defined by the *Heller* decision in 2008. Not surprisingly, the Court overturned the discretion which New York State licensing authorities can use to determine the issuance of CCW, a practice known as 'may issue,' to distinguish it from what is referred to as 'shall issue' which requires an automatic granting of CCW to individuals who are legally allowed to purchase and own guns.

Despite the fact that the minority in this case cited numerous studies which showed that gun violence has been increasing over the last decade, the dissenting opinion could not cite any specific proof of a connection between CCW and gun violence, nor for that matter do studies which show higher rates of gun violence in states with less-restrictive gun laws actually demonstrate any causal connection between regulatory practices and gun violence, if only because violent criminality is multi-causal to the extreme.

What separates and differentiates pro-gun organizations from gun-control organizations are two basic factors, one being the question of how Americans deal with the whole issue of government regulations and government activity in the first place, the second being the manner in which the two categories of organizations differ in terms of how they inform and energize their members to promote organizational responses to the issue of guns. Let's look at the second factor first.

Until the 2012 Sandy Hook massacre, the few gun-control organizations did not define themselves in terms of membership activities, and confined their work overwhelmingly to addressing political and legal issues through lobbying efforts in Washington, D.C. Despite the fact that prior to 2012 the Federal Government had enacted a total of three gun laws, whereas hundreds of gun laws exist in every state and in many localities within the states, there was no active, organizational efforts to reduce gun violence, even though gun crimes and gun assaults abounded in many locations, particularly with the surge in criminality associated with the proliferation of illegal drugs coterminous with the Viet Nam war.

The first, sustained effort to develop a mass-based, national organization to promote efforts to reduce gun violence emerged in 2000, when a barely-functioning lobbying effort known as Handgun Control, Inc., was taken over and renamed the Brady Campaign to Prevent Gun Violence which had originally been formed to push through the Brady Bill introduced in 1988 and signed by President Clinton in 1994.

Beginning in 2000, the Brady organization began to promote gun-control initiatives at the state level, as well as developing a limited effort to foster ongoing social and political activities by these state-level groups.

I attended two of these Brady meetings in my state – Massachusetts – in 2016, both of which were held in public libraries of upper-class Boston suburbs whose residents no doubt conformed to the profile of gun-control activists which I describe in the survey discussed above (pp. 124 *et. seq.*) The meetings were held on weekend afternoons, they were attended by 50 – 100 persons, and the programs of both events consisted of a welcome speech by the Brady organizer, then an emotional and depressing description of a shooting either by the mother or another family member of the victim, then a Q and A, and then the audience could attack a table of pot-luck snacks.

The speakers whose family members had been shot were, of course, Black. I say 'of course' because I doubt if there had been any shooting event of any kind at any time in the two suburbs where Brady held these events. It goes without saying that the potluck snacks were sparse, and I would estimate that within 20 minutes or so after the speeches came to an end, the room had cleared out.

These events were not enjoyable, they were not fun, and they certainly were not planned to create any degree of social interaction by the audience which showed up. The whole point of these events was to solicit individuals to join the Brady organization, which meant filling out a card with your name, address, and email, then sticking the card in an envelope along with a check.

The second national gun-control organization, Mayors Against Illegal Guns, was founded in 2006 by Mike Bloomberg, with some input from Tom Menino, at the time Mayor of Boston. The same year he founded this organization which was an effort to promote more awareness about gun violence in urban locations, Bloomberg also sued 27 gun dealers in states outside of New York whose slipshod sales practices resulted in substantial numbers of guns from their inventories ending up being used as crime guns in on New York City streets.

Most of these suits were settled out of court, several provoked counter-suits by gun dealers, but this activity put Bloomberg squarely in the middle of gun-control activities, a position which he continues through the present day. Neither the Mayors group nor Bloomberg's next organizational effort, Everytown, which Bloomberg started up in 2013, focused on building a membership base, nor did Brady's efforts to promote grass-activitics in various state localities result in any major growth of a grass-roots membership which could challenge the outreach or strength of the several million gun owners who support the NRA.

As I briefly discussed in the Introduction, the NRA's dominance in grass-roots organizational activities related to guns was finally threatened and in certain circumstances eclipsed by the work of Shannon Watts, whose MOMS group connected up with Bloomberg's Everytown effort and has used the Everytown cash flow to build a serious, grass-roots movement which operates on a regular basis in most of the fifty states.

A glance at the MOMS website reveals that the organization will be holding some kind of event in 40 of the 50 states over July, August, and September 2022. Together the website contains information about 93 events, which is a very impressive spread for an organization that didn't exist until 2013. On the other hand, when I went to the NRA website and did a search for events which are taking place just within 100 miles of where I live, the search turned up 193 events, and this is in a part of the United States which is not particularly pro-gun.

There was a second and even more important difference between the event calendars of the NRA and MOMS, namely, that the NRA events were a combination of training classes and social get-togethers at shooting ranges and gun shops. The MOMS calendar was filled with events which were basically monthly business meetings of statewide groups with an occasional political demonstration or public march thrown in.

As for building an organizational image, the MOMS website has an online store where you can purchase some 40 items with the group's logo, most of them t-shirts or a coffee mug for the home or car. The NRA store is not just a page on the organization's website, it's a complete shopping experience with all kinds of different product lines, a sign-up to receive alerts about new products and a clothing selection whose products are very fashionable, very well made and not at all cheap. Their golf polo shirts, of which I own a pair, cost as much as shirts sold by Orvis, and if anything, are better made.

The NRA has also gotten back into member benefit programs which were cancelled several years ago when the group had the big fight between Wayne LaPierre and Oliver North. Now if you are an NRA member, you not only receive a monthly magazine, but you can join the cigar club, the wine club or the coffee club and purchase travel insurance or insurance to protect your guns.

The website also has a well-designed Travel Center where you plug in your NRA membership number, then list the location of your trip and the dates. To test this process, I pretended I was going to stay overnight at Fort

Wayne, IN and the website brought up 18 motels and hotels with discounts running between 5% and 50%.

Gun-control groups like MOMS and Brady use the term 'member' in some of their correspondence when they solicit for cash, but there really is no membership category or activity at all. Not only does the NRA hold a three-day, national show every year that attracts thousands of members, many of whom make a point of getting together with other members who they first met at previous shows, but they also have a booth and a presence at hundreds of gun shows every month in all the lower 48 states.

Finally, and most important is the comparison between how the NRA solicits donations versus how groups like MOMS and Brady chase monetary contributions both through the regular mail and online. I usually donate at least $250 to the NRA each year, which makes me a member of the Golden Eagles club. What do I get for being a member of this club? I receive a nice, little plastic ID wallet card which I can show to a cop if I get stopped for speeding or going through a red light. I also get a little lapel pin which I can affix to my NRA hat. I also receive at least one snail-mail letter from Wayne LaPierre each month and often as many as one email every week.

What do I receive from MOMS and Brady for the $1,200 I give each organization every year? Occasionally I receive an email asking for an additional donation which is the same email which goes out to everyone else on their donor/prospect list. I also receive one or two solicitation letters each year, but I receive no communication of any kind acknowledging my annual donation or the fact that I have probably given both organizations at least ten thousand dollars over the past ten years.

Being a member of the NRA embraces a whole set of activities and programs which have little, if anything to do with the actual transfer of funds from my wallet to the NRA's bank account. In fact, the whole issue of a monetary relationship between NRA members and the NRA organization is very much secondary to the ways in which the NRA communicates to its members and the degree to which supporting the organization financially is taken for granted and hardly even mentioned in communications sent out on a timely and frequent basis by the NRA.

There is also a personal element which binds the NRA together with its members which is driven home by the online presence of the organization's Executive Vice President, Wayne LaPierre. When all the nasty news came out several years ago about how LaPierre was spending lots of money on private jets, exclusive hotels, and designer clothing from a boutique on Rodeo Drive, the media endlessly predicted that he would be terminated or in some way pushed out or aside.

This year, 2022, LaPierre was re-elected Executive Vice President at the annual meeting, and to most of the organization's members his continued tenure for more than 30 years came as little surprise. There were a few complaints about LaPierre's behavior and a few (but not many) resignations from the Board, along with a slight drop in overall membership numbers over the last several years.

But the reason the membership did not rise up *en masse* and demand that LaPierre be replaced was a testament to the degree that LaPierre has personalized his relationship to the membership to a degree which does not exist in any other advocacy effort which exists today in the United States. Aside from my NRA membership, I am also a member, or at least a regular financial supporter of Everytown, Brady, Audubon Society, Wilderness Society, National Park Foundation, and the AAA. If I bumped into the heads of any of those organizations, I wouldn't have the slightest idea that the money I give them every year helps pay the salary of the person whom I had just met.

On the other hand, I have not only said hello to Wayne LaPierre as he stands at the entrance to the annual show and greets everyone coming through the doors, but the NRA website always carries a video message from Wayne which usually plays as the site opens up. The letters I receive in the snail mail come from him, the emails and text messages from the NRA are also signed by him. This personal connection between Wayne LaPierre and the NRA membership is probably the primary reason the organization continues to play such a dominant role in the national gun debate.

Now let's look at the second factor which defines and separates the two sides in the discussion about guns, a factor which is just as important, or perhaps even more important than the way in which gun 'rights' groups and gun-control groups build and operate their membership base. This factor can perhaps best be summed up with the following question: what should the role of government be when it comes to owning and using guns?

The NRA refers to itself as 'America's oldest civil rights organization,' but the term 'civil rights' usually means something having to do with how government defines and enforces personal or institutional behavior. The gun-owning community, comprised of a majority of politically and religiously conservative individuals who are found most frequently in Southern states or the rural parts of Midwestern states, has always held what is at best an ambivalent view of the national state, an ambivalence which hardens into a more determined, anti-government attitude when either or both of the executive and legislative branches are controlled the Democratic Party. In fact, the exact, same voting alignment and party division which appeared when the federal government passed the civil rights act in 1964 reappeared again when the major gun law was passed in 1968.

As a result of this basic division between the liberal belief that government authority should be relied upon to define and enforce public behaviors of all kinds, whereas conservatives maintain a basic mistrust of government intervention in social affairs, the division within the gun debate breaks down into competing and contrasting strategies for how to define and deal with the role of government as regards the ownership of guns.[53]

I can perhaps best describe this division of outlook and activities by what happened in Vermont when the state government first initiated an effort to enact the state's very first gun law, Vermont being the only one of the fifty states at that time to have no statewide gun regulations on the books at all.

The day the state Senate held a public debate on the gun bill, which was March 18, 2015, the chamber's visitor's gallery had every, single seat filled, mostly by gun owners who came to show support for Senate members who were opposed to the bill. According to observers, the only previous time the entire gallery did not have an empty sear was when the Senate held its first public debate on a same-sex marriage bill in 2009. In the latter instance, the seats were overwhelmingly filled by visitors who supported such a bill.

The same-sex marriage bill passed in 2009, the 2015 gun-control bill failed. Vermont did enact a statewide gun law in 2018, but Vermont not only has no specific licensing requirement for concealed-carry but is the only state of all 50 states which does not distinguish between concealed and open carry of guns. Had a provision which required licensing for carrying firearms outside the home been attached to the 2018 bill, the legislation would have certainly failed.

It needs to be pointed out that from 2016 through 2020 of all 50 states, only Maine has a lower gun-homicide rate than Vermont. Yet most of the states with the highest rates of gun violence, particularly Southern states, only support government intervention into the issue of gun ownership when it comes to punishing individuals who commit crimes with guns. As for the law-abiding gun owner in pro-gun Southern and Midwestern states, any attempt to enact gun regulations is seen as an unwelcome intrusion of government into what is considered to be a private affair.[54]

Given these clear and sharp differences between the outlook and strategies of the two sides, what should activists and advocates do who want to see gun violence disappear the way other threats to public health like polio and dirty water have disappeared?

First and foremost, the gun-control community should stop pretending they support gun 'rights' but just want guns to be 'safe.' The guns which account for most, if not almost all the fatal and non-fatal instances of gun violence every year are not designed to be 'safe.' In fact, if a gun is designed to be used in a 'safe' manner, such as shooting only one round at a time with a manual reloading action after each round, or having a long barrel to make the gun both steadier to aim as well as making it more accurate in terms of the placement of the shot, then this is a gun which is not going to be used for the kind of shooting behavior that kills and injures on average more than 325 Americans every day.

The gun-control community does not gain any support at all from gun owners when they pledge allegiance to any kind of gun 'rights.' As long as someone like Mike Bloomberg or any of his political allies are associated with any kind of effort to reduce gun violence, the odds that some kind of positive, working relationship can be formed between the two sides in the gun debate aren't small or slight, they are nil. I don't like tobacco and I don't like full-calorie drinks. As far as I am concerned, we could do without both. And I am not about to support any program or plan which places a few more restrictions on the use of such products just because someone else likes to 'light up a Lucky' because it just feels good.

I also believe that gun-control organizations should spend more time and money making their supporters feel that being involved with a gun-control organization means something more than just throwing some bucks in that direction or discussing when to make the next trip to the State House to walk around with a placard which reads something about how gun violence has to end.

What's wrong with putting together some social events with some live music and decent food? What's wrong with spending an afternoon with other people who share concerns about gun violence but just want to hang out and have a good time? And by the way, would it be so terrible to have a website store which sells some decent clothing or other products that I can buy or give as gifts?

In 2020-2021 the Brady campaign raised $10 million in cash. Obviously, their donor base has some extra dough. They couldn't spend it on a nice jacket or a pair of slacks? Brady's website doesn't even have a page where you can buy anything at all.

Finally, and I have saved this recommendation for last because it is the most difficult but therefore the most important strategic initiative for dealing with the violence caused by guns. The fundamental argument made by gun-control activists which connects our high rate of gun violence to the existence of 300 million to 400 million privately-owned guns, as I have discussed previously, is not correct. Or at least the numbers utilized to make the argument are not correct for the simple reason that at least eighty percent of all intentional fatal and non-fatal gun injuries involve types of guns – semi-automatic, bottom-loading rifles and handguns – which only account for a part of the civilian arsenal in the United States.

If we were to calculate the number of gun-violence events which occur involving distinct racial categories – White, Black, all others – the differential between White and Black would be extreme, perhaps a difference of four times greater among Blacks as opposed to Whites, perhaps even more. If we were to pull Black gun deaths out of the overall rate and compare the remaining U.S. gun-violence rate to the rate in other advanced countries, the U.S. would no longer lead the OECD by 7 to 20 times, it's gun-violence rate would situate the country somewhere in the middle of the OECD.

In effect, the U.S. experiences two very distinct types of gun violence. One type, which is sporadic, usually involving older White males who live in isolated or smaller communities and commit gun violence against themselves. At least 120,000 individuals have committed suicide using a gun between 2016 and 2020 and the states which register the highest rates are Western and Mountain states like Alaska, Idaho, Montana, and Wyoming, with gun-suicide rates that are five times higher than states like New York, New Jersey, Massachusetts, and Rhode Island, where communities are more urban, less dispersed and access to mental health services are somewhat more advanced.

The other type of gun violence is when someone uses a gun to try to kill someone else, which has resulted in more than 75,000 fatalities over the same five years, with the statewide rates of fatal shootings of inner-city Black residents often more than ten times the rate of fatal shootings of White residents. This extreme difference in homicide rates based on race is particularly a factor in Louisiana, Alabama, and Mississippi, as well as in certain northern inner-city Black communities like St. Louis, Missouri and Chicago, Illinois.

In addition to the two different types of gun violence differentiated by location and race, there is a third difference between the two types which may be the most important difference of all. Overwhelmingly, the individuals who use a gun to end their own lives have access to a weapon which is legally owned either by themselves or someone else in the household. The states which impose specific licensing for handgun sales as a way to prevent impulsive purchase and use of guns by individuals experiencing severe mental distress, for the most part do not show any significant difference in gun-suicide rates before or after such permit-to-purchase laws go into effect. If nothing else, this is an indication that most individuals who commit gun suicide use a gun that they previously owned, usually for decades or multiple years.

This is certainly not the case with guns that figure in homicides, with the exception of homicides that are domestic events, which represent roughly 15 percent of all murders committed with guns. To begin, more than 15,000 individuals who committed murders with guns from 2016 through 2022 are under the age of 19, so they cannot legally own a gun. Many, if not most of the older offenders have been previously convicted of a felony which also removes them from the pool of individuals who can get legal access to gun before committing a capital crime. Finally, many of the guns picked up by the cops in criminal circumstances were trafficked into the particular location from other states.

How should we attempt to prevent or at least discourage access to illegal guns in the inner city, particularly in neighborhoods which seem to exhibit high and/or continuous demand for such guns? First, I do not believe that gun-control organizations should be advocating programs to deal with the 'root causes' of violence like lack of jobs, homelessness, educational deficits or any of the other social or economic conditions which exist in every inner-city disenfranchised neighborhood and no doubt play a role in shaping the culture and attitudes of inner-city residents, particularly when it comes to the circulation of illegal drugs.[55]

If members of gun-control organizations want to expand their efforts ad energies into other advocacy activities, nobody should be made to feel that there should be any barriers placed in their way of working for better lives and living experiences for all. But the main focus of groups that want to bring an end to gun violence must be a focus on the specific condition which makes gun violence an event that kills and injures more than 125,000 Americans every year, and that specific condition happens to be the presence of a gun.

My recommendation is that every jurisdiction which experiences gun violence should create a map where these events are most likely to occur and declare the area to be a 'gun free zone.' There should be signage posted where it can be easily and frequently seen and messaging should go out over all media venues – internet, radio, TV, handhelds – stating clearly and forcefully that being in possession of an illegal gun in a gun-free zone area will result in serious jail time.

Another strategy which should be implemented is a program which doesn't offer gift cards if individuals turn in guns, although a continuous gun buyback program should be put into effect at all times. What I would like to see, however, as a means of really disrupting inner-city, illegal gun ownership, is an incentive program where individuals are paid serious money, a premium amount, for alerting the authorities to the existence of illegal guns.

We conduct these kinds of citizen-response programs about serious crimes all the time. When it comes to gun violence, why not make the effort before a crime occurs? And there is nothing which prevents a police team from using a citizen's anonymous tip about an illegal gun to be given a search warrant to be executed in proper and legal fashion if there is a suspicion that a certain residence or apartment contains illegal guns.

This is the kind of strategy which gun-control groups should be spending more time planning and promoting and less time pushing lawmakers to pass yet another statute aimed at making law-abiding gun owners obey yet another law.[56] And a program which made a tangible attempt to take guns out of the hands of individuals who do not have the legal privilege to have access to a gun would generate major support from everyone engaged in the gun debate.

Imagine the following scenario. The city of Chicago offers one thousand dollars for a tip about the existence of an illegal semi-automatic pistol. Over the next several weeks, 100 guns are picked up which otherwise might ed up being used in a homicide or other violent crime. So, the authorities have just spent $100,000 but if just 10 of those guns would have otherwise not been used in a fatal assault, the state of Illinois just saved $5.5 million dollars over the next year.

What this plan reflects is the degree to which certain communities, largely poor and largely comprised of minority residents represent a market for a certain product, illegal guns, where demand is very high. How do you change the way a market operates and has been operating over time? You redesign the financial underpinnings of how that market functions in a way that shifts the financial rewards of successful market involvement away from the group whose market activity creates community-wide risks.

Endnotes

Introduction

1 To better prepare myself for these interviews, as well as to evaluate responses from the interview subjects, I read, Alan J. Lizotte, Marvin D. Krohn, James C. Howell, Kimberly Tobin and Gregory J. Howard, "Factors Influencing Gun Carrying Among Young Urban Males Over the Adolescent-Young Adult Life Course," *Criminology*, Vol. 38, 3 (2000), pp. 811-834. I also prepared myself to better understand gun violence as a medical issue by reading Peter M Rhee, Ernest E Moore, Bellal Joseph, Andrew Tang, Viraj Pandit and Gary Vercruysse, "Gunshot wounds: A review of ballistics, bullets, weapon and myths," *Journal of Trauma and Acute Care Surgery*, Vol. 80, No. 6 (June 2016), pp. 853-867.

2 The description of the Sandy Hook mass shooting is taken from contemporary media reports, as well as from the official Connecticut State report released by the Governor's office in 2015. You can download a draft copy of that report here: https://mikethegunguy.social/wp-content/uploads/2022/06/sady-hook-report.pdf.

3 The Virginia Tech shooting was described in detail in a state report issued in 2009 that can be downloaded here: https://mikethegunguy.social/wp-content/uploads/2022/06/VA-Tech-report.pdf.

4 No official report was ever issued after the Mandalay Bay shooting. Our text is based on countless media reports.

5 There was a brief flurry of media interest in comparing the frequency of mass shootings in the United States versus other countries following an offhand remark made by President Obama in June 2014 when he lamented not being able to pass a gun-control law. The public debate about the frequency of mass shootings in the United States briefly became a fixture in the national media when *The New York Times* ran a lengthy article on this subject in the November 8, 2017, edition based on research by Adam Lankford, a criminologist at the University of Alabama, who compared mass shootings in 171 countries and ranked the United States near the top of the list.

6 G. Newton and F. Zimring, *Firearms and American Life: A Staff Report to the National Commission on the Causes and Prevention of Violence* (Washington, D.C.: Government Printing Office, 1970). This report was the first attempt to develop a comprehensive count of the number of civilian-owned firearms which had been manufactured and sold since 1890 but the authors were unable to make a definitive finding because much of the data from gun manufacturers whose businesses had shut down could no longer be accessed or even found.

7 Many of the contemporary comments which appear in this book can be found in open-source news media, particularly websites of the major TV networks (NBC, CBS, ABC, FOX) and websites of major print newspapers (*The New York Times*, *Wall Street Journal*). I will cite such sources by name and date, specific pagination article titles can be searched online.

8 In March 2000, the Clinton Administration announced an agreement with Smith & Wesson in which the gun maker not only agreed to add additional safety features to all their models, but to conduct an annual safety inspection of every dealer who stocked just one Smith & Wesson new gun. Additionally, gun dealers had to show that all their employees had taken safety and compliance courses developed by the ATF as well as refresher courses whenever gun laws changed. There was simply no way that most dealers could comply with these regulations, and the agreement between Smith & Wesson and the government effectively disappeared after the 2000 election and the change of Presidential administrations from Democratic to GOP control. During the 2016 Presidential campaign, Hillary Clinton made comments which appeared to suggest that if she were elected, she would promote the 2000 gun-control plan again.

9 The NRA's recent travails are summarized, perhaps a little too forcefully, by Tim Mak, *Misfire – Inside the Downfall of the NRA* (New York: Dutton, 2021). After detailing how the NRA has been challenged and wounded by attacks both from advocacy groups and public officials, the book ends with his prescient remark: "To study the NRA is to see its remarkable resilience in the face of near bankruptcy, condemnation, scandal and internal dissension." Had the author not published his work until 2022 instead of 2021, he might have underscored his judgement about the NRA's resilience, because not only was Wayne LaPierre re-elected Executive Vice President for another three-year term, but the attempt by New York State's Attorney General to shut down the organization was blocked by a state court.

Chapter 1

10 Readers wishing to know the history and background of the Springfield Armory should consult F. Deyrup, *Arms Makers of the Connecticut Valley: A Regional Study of the Economic Development of the Small Arms Industry, 1798-1870* (Northampton, Mass.: Smith College Studies in History, vol. 33, 1948), which describes the origins and activities of the numerous machining and metal fabricating operations which together formed the industrial environment that furnished the Springfield Arsenal with finished parts and materials for its gun making operation, and D. Hounshell, *From the American System to Mass Production, 1800-1932, The Development of Manufacturing Technology in the United States* (Baltimore: The Johns Hopkins University Press, 1984) which

details the design and performance of machinery which allowed for the transformation of manufacturing from hand production to mass production of metal and wooden small arms components.

11 In 1981 the Republicans submitted legislation to "protect firearms owners' constitutional rights, civil liberties, and rights of privacy," and held 3 public hearings on Senate 1030, which never went to a Senate vote. Nevertheless, the entire transcript of the hearings has been published and makes substantive reading about GCA68, cf., United States Congress, *The Firearms Owners Protection Act* (Ann Arbor, University of Michigan Library, 2014.)

12 G. Kleck and M. Gertz, "Armed Resistance to Crime: The Prevalence and Nature of Self-Defense with a Gun," *Journal of Criminal Law and Criminology*, Vol. 86, no. 1 (Fall, 1995), pp. 150-186.

13 Kellermann A.L., Rivara F.P., Somes G., Reay D.T., Francisco J., Banton J.G., Prodzinski J., Fligner C., Hackman B.B., "Suicide in the Home in Relation to Gun Ownership," *New England Journal of Medicine* 327 (August 13, 1992), 467-472; Kellermann A.L., Rivara F.P., Rushforth N.B., Banton J.G., Reay D.T., Francisco J.T., Locci A.B., Prodzinski J., Hackman B.B., Somes G., "Gun Ownership as a Risk Factor for Homicide in the Home," *New England Journal of Medicine* 329 (October 7, 1993), pp. 1084-1091.

14 Hemenway and colleagues have conducted, published, and updated this evidence multiple times. Here is one of the latest efforts: Hemenway D. and Grinshteyn E, "Violent death rates: the United States compared to other high-Income OECD Countries," *American Journal of Medicine.* 129 (2016) pp. 266-73.

15 Weisser, Michael, "Understanding Guns and Gun Violence," *SSRN* (September 17, 2018).

16 J. Lott, *More Guns, Less Crime. Understanding Crime and Gun-Control Laws* (Chicago, University of Chicago Press, 1998). The book has one through multiple editions, for the most part being used by the author to respond to much of the criticism that the book has received. Also see, Brian Anse Patrick, *Rise of the Anti-Media: In-forming America's Concealed Weapons Carry Movement* (London: Artkos, 2013). This self-published book is a brilliant analysis of how social media was used by pro-gun groups outside of the 'established' gun 'rights' community to promote concealed-carry and armed, self-defense.

17 Siegel M., Xuan Z., Ross C.S., Galea S., Kalesan B., Fleegler E., Goss K.A., "Easiness of Legal Access to Concealed Firearm Permits and Homicide Rates in the United States," *American Journal of Public Health*, Vol. 107, 12 (December 2017), pp. 1923-1929.

Chapter 2

18 See the article in The Trace by Jennifer Mascia and Chip Brownlee, "Thirty-two States Let People Carry Guns without Learning How to Shoot One," https://www.thetrace.org/2022/01/which-states-require-firearm-safety-course-concealed-carry/.

19 L. Adelson, "The gun and the sanctity of human life; or the bullet as pathogen," *Archives of Surgery*, 127 (June 1992), pp.659-664. The quote is from p. 667.

20 M. Wolfgang, *Patterns of Criminal Homicide,* Philadelphia: University of Pennsylvania Press, 1958.

21 FBI-UCR, "*2019 Crime in the United States*," Expanded Homicide Data Table 10.

22 The Department of Justice report which was based on interviews with more than 50 witnesses could not find any basis on which to indict the police officer who shot and killed Brown. You can download the report here: https://mikethegunguy.social/wp-content/uploads/2022/06/doj_report_on_ shooting_of_michael_brown _1.pdf.

Chapter 3

23 All of the ATF's data on tracing and other regulatory activities can be found here: Data & Statistics | Bureau of Alcohol, Tobacco, Firearms and Explosives (atf.gov).

24 Much of this section is based on a detailed, 534-page report about the Waco siege published by the Department of the Treasury in September 1993. This report can be downloaded here: https://mikethegunguy.social/wp-content/uploads/2022/06/WACO-Report.pdf. None of the books published on Waco contain he degree of detail found in this report.

25 Almost as compelling as the Waco report is the 2012 DoJ report on Fast and Furious, which can be downloaded here: https://mikethegunguy.social/wp-content/uploads/2022/06/WACO-Report.pdf. A solid book on this subject is Mike Detty, *Guns across the Border, The Inside Story* (New York: Skyhorse Publishing, 2013).

26 The CAP report can be downloaded here: https://mikethegunguy.social/wp-content/uploads/2022/06/WACO-Report.pdf.

Chapter 4

27 Cf., Deborah Azrael, Lisa Hepburn, David Hemenway, and Matthew Miller., "The Stock and Flow of U.S. Firearms: Results from the 2015 National Firearms

Survey," *RSF: The Russell Sage Foundation Journal of the Social Sciences*, Vol. 3, No. 5 (October 2017), pp. 38-57.

28 Information on manufacturing of guns by type of weapon are published annually by ATF and can be accessed on the ATF website.

29 Pictures and text about NRA advertisements are drawn from a slightly overdone article in *Mother Jones:* Gilson, Dave, "This Collection of NRA Ads Reveals Its Descent into Crazy" *Mother Jones*, April 10, 2013.

30 Carter P.M., Walton M.A., Newton M.F., Clery M., Whiteside L.K., Zimmerman M.A., Cunningham R.M., "Firearm Possession among Adolescents Presenting to an Urban Emergency Department for Assault," *Pediatrics*, Vol. 132, No. 2 (August 2013), pp. 213-221.

31 Cf., *The New York Times*, May 11, 2007, covering a story about a law passed in Virginia that would prohibit Bloomberg from sending agents into gun shops because only federal or state personnel can enforce gun laws in a particular state.

32 Cf., https://www.supremecourt.gov/qp/12-01493qp.pdf which covers the questions that were used by the Supreme Court to grant certiorari.

33 Emmanuel Le Roy Ladurie, *Les paysans de Languedoc* [*The Peasants of Languedoc*] (Paris: Editions Flammarion, 1977.)

34 https://www.sunshinebehavioralhealth.com/blog/usa-war-on-drugs-info-cost/.

35 https://concealedcarrykillers.org/.

36 This was reported to me by members of the Johns Hopkins Center for Gun Violence Prevention and Policy, but publication is embargoed so I cannot provide specific details for public access to this research.

37 Cf., https://news.gallup.com/poll/179213/six-americans-say-guns-homes-safer.aspx.

Chapter 5

38 When I started writing about gun violence, I realized that my knowledge about guns was much greater than my knowledge about the medical issues surrounding gun violence. In particular, I possessed only fragmentary, superficial knowledge about the medical effects of gun injuries and the circumstances in which gun violence occurred. Some information was available in various data collections of the CDC and the FBI, but what became my basic source for understanding the total context in which a gun assault occurs came from L. Adelson, *The Pathology of Homicide – A Vade Mecum for Pathologist, Prosecutor and Defense Counsel* (Springfield, IL, Thomas Books, 1974), a thousand-page classic which has served as the basic reference work for medical and legal specialists in this particular field.

39 Unfortunately, for reasons of protecting privacy, access to the detailed data in NVDRS is restricted to individuals who must first request the use of this information through a tedious application process designed to keep everyone but

the most academically-endowed researchers unable to take advantage of this important data source.

40 Crifasi C.K., Meyers J.S., Vernick J.S., Webster D.W., "Effects of Changes in permit-to-purchase handgun laws in Connecticut and Missouri on suicide rates," *Preventive Medicine*, 2015, 79 (October 2015) pp. 43-49.

41 Azrael D., Cohen J., Salhi C., Miller M., "Firearm Storage in Gun-Owning Households with Children: Results of a 2015 National Survey," *Journal of Urban Health*, Vol. 95 (May 10, 2018) pp. 295-304.

Chapter 6

42 Cf., for a discussion of Constitutional 'rights' Louis Fisher and David Adler, *American Constitutional Law, Vol. 2, Civil Rights and Civil Liberties* (Durham, Caroline Academic Press, 2007) and Eric Foner, *The Second Founding, How the Civil War and Reconstruction Remade the Constitution* (New York, Norton, 2019).

43 https://www.pewresearch.org/social-trends/2017/06/22/the-demographics-of-gun-ownership/. The full report can be downloaded here: https://mikethegunguy.social/wp-content/uploads/2022/06/Guns-Report-FOR-WEBSITE-PDF-6-21.pdf.

44 S. Levinson, "The Embarrassing 2nd Amendment," *The Yale Law Journal,* Vol. 99 (1989), pp. 637- 659. You can download it here: https://mikethegunguy.social/wp-content/uploads/2022/06/LEVINSON.pdf.

45 Full text of the Heller decision: https://mikethegunguy.social/wp-content/uploads/2022/06/Heller.pdf.

Chapter 7

46 L. Klarevas, *Rampage Nation: Securing America from Mass Shootings,* New York, Prometheus Books, 2016.

47 I am not citing media sources for any of these shootings because in each instance there was intense media coverage which can easily be accessed online.

48 The FBI report can be downloaded here: https://mikethegunguy.social/wp-content/uploads/2022/06/U_ActiveShooter021317_17B_WEB.pdf.

49 In addition to contemporary media accounts, the description of what occurred in the Norway rampage is based primarily on the detailed psychiatric report issued by the court in 2012, along with the government's indictment document which is reproduced here: *Anders Behring Breivik: the indictment | Anders Breivik | The Guardian.*

50 Vella M.A., Warshauer A., Tortorello G., Fernandez-Moure J., Giacolone J., Chen B., Cabulong A., Chreiman K., Sims C., Schwab C.W., Reilly P.M., Lane-Fall M., Seamon M.J., "Long-term Functional, Psychological, Emotional, and Social Outcomes in Survivors of Firearm Injuries." *JAMA Surgery*, Vol. 155, 1 (November 20, 2019), pp. 51-59.

51 Data on mass shootings collected by the ALERRT program can be found here: ALERRT Active Attack Data - Home.

Chapter 8

52 Cf., the summary of extensive research on gun shows by Garen Wintemute: IGSexecsummweb.pdf (ucdavis.edu). Wintemute presents an overall analysis of the population which attends gun shows: "The demographic homogeneity at some shows, particularly in the Midwest, is remarkable. Well under 10 percent of those present are other than white males, and most of these men appear to be well over 50 years of age." (p. 7.) This description of the gun show attendees also is no different from the general profile of gun owners.

Conclusion

53 The difference between the two advocacy positions about guns is invariably described as a difference between how conservatives versus liberals view the role of government in terms of social controls. But this issue deserves to be studied on a more detailed level, as suggested by D. Braman and D. Kahan, "More Statistics, Less Persuasion: A Cultural Theory of Gun-Risk Perceptions," *Yale Law School, Public Law & Legal Theory, Working Paper 05.* The authors argue persuasively that the conservative-liberal dichotomy about gun control is a function of how these two groups differ on the issue of governmental response to risk.

54 The shift towards linking programs to reduce gun violence to program that will reduce socio-economic deprivation in poor neighborhoods has become a standard narrative within the gun-control community. Cf., a report issued by the Joyce Foundation, "Toward a Fair and Just Response to Gun Violence,' based on meetings which brought together more than 30 experts in the fields of criminal justice, gun violence research, advocates, policy, violence intervention and law enforcement to craft 'consensus' recommendations to reduce gun violence. To expand violence interventions, the report calls for "improving economic mobility, access to safe and affordable housing, and access to healthcare for returning residents through increased collaboration between community violence intervention and reentry stakeholders." (Cf. T*oward-a-Fair-and-Just-Response-*

to-Gun-Violence-II.pdf (joycefdn.org)). In other words, what we need is a domestic version of the Marshall Plan, as if such an effort is: a) politically feasible, and b) would immunize violence-prone individuals to resort to less violent behavior.

An article which covers the process utilized in Israel to determine an individual's fitness to carry a concealed weapon describes an evaluation process of such length and complexity that the idea of replicating such a procedure in any American jurisdiction boggles the mind. *Cf.,* Melamed Y., Bauer A., Kalian M., Rosca P., Mester R., "Assessing the Risk of Violent Behavior Before Issuing a License to Carry a Handgun," *Journal of the Academy of Psychiatry and Law*, Vol. 39 (2011), pp. 543-548.

55 Research on how the illegal or what is referred to as the 'underground' gun market is limited, but this article solid research into primary/secondary sources, along with commentary from conversations between individuals who buy and sell in the underground market and an experienced undercover interviewer representing the research team. *Cf.,* P. Cook, J. Ludwig, S. Venkatesh, A. A. Braga, "Underground Gun Markets," *The Economic Journal,* Vol. 117 (November 2007), pp. F588-F618.

56 Zimring, F. "Firearms and Federal Law: The Gun Control Act of 1975" *Journal of Legal Studies*, 4 (1975) pp. 133 – 198. A detailed, authoritative, and balanced study of the strengths and limitations of federal laws for controlling gun violence.

About the Author

Michael R. Weisser was educated in NYC public schools and earned his PhD at Northwestern University in 1971 (Economic History). He taught at CCNY, University of South Carolina, University of California, Berkeley, and Columbia University. Weisser is a gun retailer, wholesaler, importer, and lethal-force instructor since 1976 and an NRA Patriot Benefactor Life Member. He is married and lives in Pelham, MA.

Name Index

R

S

T

W

Subject Index